The End of Liberalism

Other Books of Interest from St. Augustine's Press

Patrick J. Deneen, *Conserving America?: Essays on Present Discontents*

Roger Kimball, *The Fortunes of Permanence:
Culture and Anarchy in an Age of Amnesia*

David Ramsay Steele, *Orwell Your Orwell: A Worldview on the Slab*

Zbigniew Janowski, *Homo Americanus:
The Rise of Totalitarian Democracy in America*

Taylor F. Flagg (editor), *The Long Night of the Watchman:
Essays by Václav Benda, 1977–1989*

David Lowenthal, *Slave State: Rereading Orwell's 1984*

Daniel J. Mahoney, *Recovering Politics, Civilization, and the Soul:
Essays on Pierre Manent and Roger Scruton*

Allen Mendenhall, *Shouting Softly: Lines on Law, Literature, and Culture*

Paul M. Weyrich, and William S. Lind, *The Next Conservatism*

Rémi Brague, *The Anchors in the Heavens*

Rémi Brague, *Moderately Modern*

Rémi Brague, *On the God of the Christians (and on one or two others)*

Rémi Brague, *The Legitimacy of the Human*

Jeremy Black, *The Importance of Being Poirot*

Jeremy Black, *In Fielding's Wake*

Joseph Bottum, *Spending the Winter*

Josef Pieper, *Traditional Truth, Poetry, Sacrament:
For My Mother, on her 70th Birthday*

Alexandre Kojève, *The Concept, Time, and Discourse*

Gene Fendt, *Camus' Plague: Myth for Our World*

Roger Scruton, *The Politics of Culture and Other Essays*

Roger Scruton, *The Meaning of Conservatism: Revised 3rd Edition*

Roger Scruton, *An Intelligent Person's Guide to Modern Culture*

Winston Churchill, *The River War*

The End of Liberalism
CHILTON WILLIAMSON, JR.

ST. AUGUSTINE'S PRESS
South Bend, Indiana

Manufactured in the United States of America.

1 2 3 4 5 6   28 27 26 25 24 23

Library of Congress Control Number: 2022949460

Paperback ISBN: 978-1-58731-219-9
Ebook ISBN: 978-1-58731-220-5

∞ The paper used in this publication meets the minimum
requirements of the American National Standard for Information Sciences –
Permanence of Paper for Printed Materials, ANSI Z39.48-1984.

St. Augustine's Press
www.staugustine.net

For Maureen McCaffrey Williamson

TABLE OF CONTENTS

PREFACE

Liberalism is not yet a dead faith, but it is a dying one. The word "faith" instead of "philosophy" applies here, because liberalism does not amount to a philosophy or even an "ideology" (a much over- and inaccurately-used word today, though it properly refers to the belief that all of history can be explained by reference to a secret conceptual key known only to its adepts and their followers). Liberalism is an intellectual and emotional attitude toward the world, much as conservatism is, and certainly no more highly developed systematically. Liberalism is not a theory, but *it is* a theoretical way—and a highly theoretical one at that—of looking at and understanding the world. This is the reason why, some time around the sixteenth and early seventeenth century, true philosophy—philosophy as the Greeks developed it as a means of understanding the natural world and the humanity that constitutes a part of it—was replaced by "political philosophy," which is not philosophy at all but merely political theory. In this theoretical approach to the world we find the beginnings of what Kenneth Minogue, the late scholar of political thought, called "the liberal mind." That is to say, we find the beginnings of the scientific (the theoretical) approach to understanding everything, including human beings taken individually and collectively. As scientific thought seeks to classify and generalize in order to comprehend and explain reality, the strain of political thought we call liberalism has striven to develop the concept of generic man upon which the plausibility of the liberal understanding of men depends. This concept, in company with and encouraged by parallel development of the applied sciences, made accelerating progress in the nineteenth and twentieth centuries, until by the early twenty-first century it achieved what is at once its *ne plus ultra* and its point of no return. What the author and social critic James Kalb calls "advanced liberalism" not only believes that human nature is infinitely malleable, it denies that human beings have a fixed nature at all, which amounts more or less to the same thing. From this postulate, advanced liberalism concludes that human nature—and human beings themselves—can be perfected by the technique brought to bear upon them by the natural and social sciences, and that it is the job—even the moral duty—of liberal government to coordinate this technique among scientific and political "experts" to realize results liberals want and expect. These experts know very well that it is humanly "natural" for unperfected human nature to resist their efforts to "improve" it by changing it, and therefore that the liberal utopia can be achieved only by un-democratic and anti-democratic means, and so they have been depending progressively on such means for decades now. The result is the formation of the "un-democratic liberalism" that liberals call "populism" (more commonly "right-wing populism") across Europe and in the United States.

Discussing his "legacy" in a television interview less than two weeks before leaving office, President Obama expressed confidence that "the generation behind me" will be in the majority and that under its management his liberal vision of the country will be realized. It is typical of liberals to suppose that every generation will be more liberal than the next: that liberalism, in other words, is irreversible and unstoppable. Only people ignorant of history and the nature of the human species could misunderstand the world so profoundly as that. And yet, Obama's brave talk to the contrary, Western liberals are progressively disoriented, angry, and fearful. And they are right to be. People will not tolerate forever the imposition by the liberal managerial state and its institutions of an inverted world of its own imagination in which all nations are illegitimate constructions, patriotism is out-moded and wicked, all peoples, cultures, and religions are identical, sex is a social construct, the family is an oppressive and antisocial unit of society, children in the womb are neither human nor owed protection, all truth is de-constructible, the materialist philosophy fully explains reality, and God is an illusion—in short, that black is white, and white black. Ordinary people know better than that and they are tired of either pretending not to, or going along with the pretence. And once they begin to question and react against the liberal regime and its program, and once they decide against it, the whole structure of unreality that liberalism has built up over centuries will be in peril, since the vast majority of people simply wish to be left free to lead properly human lives based on traditional, individual, social, political, and religious understandings.

Historically, liberalism has been considered the thinking man's party, conservatism that of the unreflective, unimaginative, and even ignorant reactionary. The distinction is explained by the fact that liberalism has a social as well as an intellectual aspect, owing to the success it has had in appealing to—and actually helping to make—the elite class. (Liberalism has always been a form of social, as well as of intellectual, snobbery.) Yet reality is changing, and changing fast. Most of the original and innovative thinking today is being done on the right—in America, in France, in England, even in Russia—while liberals are left with their outdated, counterfactual theories and their determination to defend them. But it will not work. Liberal theory has always been too tenuously grounded in and related to unreality to allow it to survive a mass assault of equally determined people who *feel* the truth ("in their hips," in the words of the late Willmoore Kendall, a professor of political theory at Yale). Small wonder that they should react to the contemporary rightist groundswell against them with fear, anger, and growing outrage.

* * *

"Personally, I'm still trying to figure out how to keep my anger simmering—letting it boil over won't do any good, but it shouldn't be allowed to cool. This election was an outrage, and we should never forget it," wrote Paul Krugman in "The Tainted Election," his *New York Times* article for 11 December 2016.

Paul Krugman, a liberal economist and journalist, does not attempt to disguise the fear, anger, and despair he feels following the events of November 8. The anger is as unjustified as that of a conservative commentator following the presidential elections of 2008 and 2012 would have been—but the fear and despair are wholly justified.

The post-war Western world is drawing to its end after more than seven decades. It is the world modern liberalism made in reaction to its own history stretching back more than two centuries and to the history of the first half of the 20th century: the world of liberal internationalism and liberal democracy accompanied by high-minded interventionism, democratic capitalism and the corporate state, first civil, then human, rights tending toward extreme individualism, the expansion of globalist economics, the weakening of the nation state, and migrations from the Third World to the First. In the last 30 years it has also been the world of anti-Western multiculturalism, advanced secularism, materialism, and relativism, deconstructionism, and a progressive program of the "disenchantment of the world" (Max Weber's phrase) facilitated by these things, as well by an increasingly technological, bureaucratic, and managerial society. Finally, the liberal post-war world was dominated by what until 1991 was the world's sole superpower: its inspiration, creator, manager, and protector. The liberal world was substantially created by people who took America for their model, some of whom in some instances were literally paid by Washington to do so. Today both the model and the world are coming apart to make way for new, as yet unformed, and still unforeseeable replacements. The only certainty is that, contrary to Francis Fukuyama's assertion a quarter-century ago, the "end of history" did not arrive with the coming of the liberal post-war world; a fact Fukuyama himself has all but conceded in recent years.

How, and why, are liberalism and the world liberalism made collapsing, and what are the signs of their impending collapse? "Collapse" is perhaps too dramatic a word to describe a protracted historical event, yet history seems to be advancing faster in this era of mass digital communications, mass population movements, and the coming together of unlike people, many of whom barely suspected each other's existence a century ago. And so, in the case of liberalism, "collapse" may prove to be an accurate characterization after all, though in historically relative terms.

Liberalism is described and defended by its admirers and apologists as the philosophy and social-political system that is not only best suited to modernity but essential to it. Liberalism is a regulatory system of economic, legal, social, educational, scientific, environmental, moral, and ethical institutions designed to manage mass industrial, technological and most recently multicultural and multiracial societies efficiently and fairly. In the age of applied psychology, liberal society is also a therapeutic society that seeks to mold, shape, and adapt its citizens to psychological standards it considers socially appropriate to a liberal environment. Thus liberal society is a controlling as well as a regulatory society, managed by presumed experts whose expressed concern for individuality and individual rights is both abstract and compromised by liberalism's commitment to the social homogeneity and intellectual agreement necessary to the smoothly efficient working of the corporate-managerial liberal state. For that reason, among others, liberalism—or "advanced liberalism," as James Kalb called it in an important book published nearly a decade ago—is a relativist persuasion that discourages and resists fixed beliefs and certainties and the idea of truth itself. Modern liberalism works from the assumption that a people who do not believe strongly in anything, people without strong beliefs, ideas, patriotic loyalties, and (above all) religions to defend will be a mild, patient, peaceable, and manageable people—provided only that they accept unquestioningly the secular and relativistic principles upon which liberalism rests.

Despite their claim to be humanists, liberals have always had an extraordinarily narrow understanding of the human person and of human society, a narrowness inevitably embodied by liberal programs and never so much as in what they call the "globalist" 21st century. It is not just that liberalism attempts to put flesh and blood people in straitjackets; it works to dehumanize them as well. Liberalism takes for granted Nietzsche's claim that God is dead, while ignoring its corollary that humanity must in that case be dead as well. Liberals cannot make God disappear. But neither can they make human nature go away. Human beings have a peculiar resistance to being forked out of their natures like *escargots* from a shell, a fact that confronts liberalism with an existential problem as Western people react at long last against the false reality liberals have tried for many generations to set up in place of the thing itself and liberalism can't imagine an alternative to its counterfeit creation. Still, as R. R. Reno, the author and editor of the magazine *First Things* observes, people need to believe in something absolutely—a need liberalism is quite unable to satisfy. Liberals do not understand this need; for them human satisfaction comes from some "self-realization" and material well-being rather than religious belief. But their inability to understand commitment to transcendent truth (religion) as something other than "reaction" (cf. *The Shipwrecked Mind: On Political Reaction* [2016] by Mark Lilla, Professor of History at Columbia University) is a fatal flaw in their makeup. Un-comprehending, they are in a state of denial regarding the appeal of Donald Trump in the United States and that of "far-right populists" like Nigel Farage and Marine Le Pen in Europe, who are far closer to old-fashioned conservatives than liberals are able to admit.

This is the meaning of what they condemn as "far-right populism" in every European country and Trumpism in the United States, electorally supported by 74 million "deplorables." This is the voice of liberal desperation speaking, yet if anything at all is certain it is that name-calling will not simply fail to halt the precipitous decline of liberalism and the liberal, it will hasten it. One of the greatest of the Left's weaknesses in the crisis is it failure to understand that what it calls "populism" is actually traditional democracy being pushed by people who are really traditional democrats. An excellent example of this want of perception and imagination is Jan-Werner Müller's *What Is Populism?* (2017), which manages to get almost everything wrong, beginning with the author's ascription of a claim of moral purity to populism and populists rather than to liberalism and liberals, for whom it is the basis of their enormous self-assurance.

CHAPTER ONE | TWO ELECTIONS

1. 2016: Rebellion

Barry Goldwater's nomination by the Republican Party as its presidential candidate at the Cow Palace in San Francisco in July, 1964, was a gallant and brilliant raid against the Party's establishment and at once a *cri de coeur* and battle cry from conservative Americans against the liberal establishment that had begun to take form in the 1930s under the New Deal. The party had consolidated its power after 1945 by converting half or more of the GOP to a moderate facsimile of itself, and by the time President Eisenhower left office in 1961 it appeared to be scarcely less than the mind and voice of America herself. Goldwater's campaign, from start to finish, was the political equivalent of the Charge of the Light Brigade; and everyone involved in it, including the 27,175, 754 million people who cast their vote for him (38.5% of the total), was aware of the fact. Few of them, indeed, can have expected their candidate to win, while voting for him anyway in a spirit of something like despair and proud defiance.

By contrast, in nominating Donald J. Trump for President 52 years later, the Republicans were keenly aware of taking a calculated risk in what was, however, considerably more than a wild gamble. The incumbent Democratic administration was unpopular after eight years, and Hillary Clinton offered no change either in character or direction from Barack Obama's White House. Further, she was a charmless and uningratiating personality with a hectoring and unpleasant demeanor on the campaign trail who was being fielded by her party for no better reason than that it had no obvious alternative, and from the assumption—encouraged by Mrs. Clinton herself—that her "turn had come" for a go at the golden ring. As for the opposing party, it was as lacking in interesting, convincing, and inspiring candidates as the Donkey Party was, composed of a sorry collection of political hacks, careerist retreads, and ideological conformists pretending to differ with one another other on a limited range of stale policies, many or most of which they had cribbed from the Democrats. Most rules, however, carry exceptions; in 2016, that exception was Donald Trump, the billionaire realtor, reality show host, political maverick and iconoclast who was saying things that tens of millions of Americans had thought for years without daring to say, and that Republican politicos (as well as Democratic ones) had spent decades hoping and expecting no candidate for political office in the United States ever *would* say. And beyond Trump's candor and political common sense lay the evident fact that between Hillary Clinton and Jeb Bush, there was almost no difference at all.

Donald Trump was a refreshing, and therefore highly popular, candidate from the beginning. Indeed, to his admirers, he seemed to rejuvenate the Republican Party, a large number—perhaps a majority—of whose members recognized an historic opportunity to challenge the dominance of its featureless establishment of gray, unimaginative, and timid placeholders, men and women without a political idea in their heads save that of winning election or re-election and continuing to enjoy the emoluments of office, and replace them with energetic and imaginative people of conviction, and the understanding and foresight to recognize where the present bipartisan liberal consensus was taking the country. There was great risk, of course, in nominating Trump. It would be a gamble and a wager, not unlike Pascal's famous theological proposition. If the party determined to make Trump their man, they had everything to gain if their decision proved the winning one; if not, their loss to Hillary Clinton left them no worse off than if the voters sent Jeb Bush or John Kasich to the White House. Indeed, the latter eventuality would prove in the end the more disastrous one, as it could only reconfirm the established GOP as the main opposition party to the Democrats, leaving the Trump Republicans with no alternative to forming a third party and running the risk of splitting the conservative and moderate-conservative vote and throwing future elections to the Donkeys.

So the Republican Party gambled—at least enough of it did—and voted to run Donald Trump for President in 2016, with what hope of winning it is impossible to say. It is probably true, however, that many Republicans went to bed on election night expecting Trump to lose, and that 2016 would be 1964 all over again. Certainly the Democrats, not least Mrs. Clinton, did. In the event, the result proved to be a case of strong heart losing fair lady—by beating her.

2. Donald Trump: Here and Abroad

I was airborne with my wife by regional jet from Laramie to Denver International Airport scarcely four hours after Hillary Clinton conceded the presidential election to Donald Trump and arrived at a little past dusk in midtown Manhattan, where 87 percent of the voters had supported the Democratic candidate. Trump Tower was already being mobbed by demonstrators and a half-riotous mob was marching north on Sixth Avenue as we checked into the hotel at West 54th Street. An hour later we were in a cab on the way to a dinner party at First Avenue and 56th. The driver was compelled by furious protesters and the large restraining police presence to detour around the Tower on Fifth Avenue between 56th and 57th through traffic as binding as an ice field. He was a dark-skinned immigrant from somewhere in Caribbean, I should have said Santo Domingo. "The election is over," the driver remarked across his shoulder through the half way open window in the bullet proof partition. "What do they think they're doing here? All these people, the media, the lies. The people who don't want to work. He's a good man— they've been so unfair to him. It's a real shame."

At dinner given us by the editor of *First Things*, R.R. Reno, and his wife, the mood was one of quiet satisfaction, even of gratitude, no matter that Thanksgiving Day was two weeks in the future. It prevailed again the following evening at Randolph's Bar in the Hotel Warwick where our guests included the late Gerald Russello, who edited *The University Bookman*, and John Carney, then an economic writer for the *Wall Street Journal* (shortly to depart for Breitbart), who reported that the editorial staff was in mourning. Later a fat Texas real estate tycoon who had been boasting of his $50,000 Patek Philippe wristwatch began to pump his arms up and down while bellowing, "*Trump! Trump! Trump!*" The large party at the table next to us joined in enthusiastically, and so did other voices around the room. I sat back and waited for the answering boos, but none came.

Two days later we boarded *Queen Mary 2* in Brooklyn for an eastbound crossing to Southampton. The ship sailed at five and we descended from the lounge to the dining saloon at 8:30, where, having misread the table assignment placed in the cabin, I was surprised to discover two couples seated at a table for six instead of a small one set for two. As we'd had bad luck with dinner companions on previous voyages I made a mental note to have a word with the *maître d'* afterward. I never did, though, because it became plain to all six of us within six minutes that we were a crossing party made in Heaven. Our new friends were an English couple in their early 50s from Taunton, near Bristol (and not far from Evelyn Waugh's two country houses in Somerset), and an American one from Tallahassee in their 60s; both well to do, the husbands being successful businessmen. The first couple were not especially knowledgeable about Trump, but they admired the man and wished him well, and husband and wife had voted Leave the previous June. The Americans had cheered Brexit from across the Pond, and were hard for Donald Trump. "We're pissed off," the Tallahassee man explained simply, and all of us drank to that. Most of the passenger list this crossing was British, few Americans were aboard; yet the other Britons we encountered around the ship were well disposed toward the results of November the eighth, and so, with a single exception of the man I encountered on the spray-soaked foredeck during a Force 8 gale, were the Americans we spoke with.

After seven nights at sea, the ship docked at Southampton at six-thirty in the morning, within sight of the quay from which *Titanic* had sailed 114 years before and where another of Cunard's *Queens* (the *Elizabeth* or the *Victoria*, I couldn't discern which through binoculars) was berthed, the early sun bright on her distinctive orange-red house colors applied to the funnel. The elegant boat trains running between Southampton Docks and Waterloo Station having been discontinued years ago, we rode a motor coach up to Victoria Bus Station in London and a black cab from there to the hotel in Grosvenor Square. London seemed far more cheerful than New York had been, despite what disgruntled Remainers were calling Brexump, or Trumpex, or some other thing—I forget what. As the car passed the roundabout at Apsley House (postal address No. 1, London; the first Duke of Wellington's former residence), the cabbie apologized for having to detour round an orderly demonstration at Hyde Park Corner. "Always something with these chappies," he remarked, and I responded, "In New York, they were all about Donald Trump." "And what do *you* think?" he asked me. "We're keen on Trump," I told him. "And we were *very* pleased by Brexit." The man nodded and gave me a wide cabbie grin backward through the partition. "Time we told them what we thought—eh?"

As a regular reader of *The Spectator*, the *Daily Telegraph*, *The Times*, and *The New Statesman* (*The Guardian* is more fun to make up for myself) I arrived in London with a pretty comprehensive sense of the British media's view of both Brexit and the President-elect. So I felt free more or less to neglect the London dailies during the five days we spent in town. Drinks with editors and correspondents for *Chronicles*, of which I was then the editor, only confirmed the situation for me. I found the British press of two minds about Donald Trump immediately following the election. For instance, a former deputy editor of *The Spectator* who has also worked at the *Telegraph*, and the current deputy at the first of these two publications, were hostile to Mr. Trump, as they had been from the start of the campaign, like many of the magazine's regular columnists. On the other hand, Charles Moore, a former editor of both *The Spectator* and the *Telegraph* (as well as Mrs. Thatcher's official biographer), had treated him with consistent sympathy in his column "The *Spectator*'s Notes" throughout the year. (*The Spectator* endorsed the Leave campaign, though rumor had it that the magazine's editor, Fraser Nelson, in private, is a Remainer.) My journalistic friends' (also colleagues') objections to Trump struck me as having less to do with issues of policy than of style, however; and I left England with the strong impression that the abiding British sense of class distinctions largely explains the man's unpopularity with the conservative intellectual class in Great Britain. Trump emphatically is *not* an ideologue; yet one can easily understand how his brash and blustering campaign style might suggest an ideological commitment behind it. As a politician Donald Trump is everything Peregrine Worsthorne, the veteran English journalist, warned no democratic politician should be; and indeed no British politician ever has been.

We arrived at Gare du Nord in Paris between the center-right *Républicain* primary election on Sunday November the twentieth, when

François Fillon, a former prime minister and Deputy for Paris in the French Assembly, handily disposed of Nicolas Sarkozy, former President of the French Republic and we departed De Gaulle Airport two days before the run-off vote on the twenty-seventh in which Fillon overwhelmed Alain Juppé, the mayor of Bordeaux (previously a one-term prime minister himself), by taking 67 percent of the vote.

On Wednesday the 23rd, four days after the first anniversary of the massacre at the Bataclan, Paris was characteristically relaxed but "*le surprise Fillon*" remained fresh in everyone's mind. As with "*le surprise Trump*" two weeks before, the victor had been favored to win by neither the pollsters nor the bookmakers. As a columnist for the left-of-center *Le Monde* explained, they failed to correctly estimate the internal forces operating within the ranks of *Les Républicains,* as their British counterparts had failed to foresee Brexit and their American ones the election of Donald Trump. Beyond that, the parallels between the primary elections in France and the presidential one in America were very marked. A writer for the conservative *Le Figaro* noted that, following Trump's electoral victory, the possibility of both the spread of "*la cause du people*" to France and Sarkozy's nomination as the presidential candidate of the French right might have been considered, but was not. Sarkozy, who in his campaign to regain the presidency had defended France's historical identity, proposed restrictions on immigration, and demanded the assimilation of the French Muslim population to the majority, was widely viewed as France's answer to Donald Trump. On the other hand, a commentator for *Le Figaro* argued against using "populism" as "*ce mot pas-partout,*" and designating as "populist" whatever one dislikes, fails to understand, and fears. "The election of Donald Trump," he wrote, "placed under the sign of protectionism and economic nationalism, has become emblematic of a global movement to halt the free-trade wave."

Throughout the campaign, Alain Juppé put himself forward as a "new man," representative of what he called the new France, while Fillon, in the role of the *conservateur* of the old one, promised to reduce immigration significantly, support traditional social norms, exercise what he called "strict administrative control" over Islam in France, and bolster the French security forces against future terrorist acts. Both men pledged to "dynamize" an economy immobilized by President François Hollande's Socialist government, a term widely understood to mean "liberalize" it. Although some critics saw the candidates' respective economic policies as convergent, Fillon proposed delivering *"un choc"* to a society stalled in so many respects on so many fronts, including by doing away with 500,000 public sector jobs, a strategy his opponent attacked as at once brutal and unrealistic and that the left denounced as "ultra-liberal." Whether convergent or not, Juppé's and Fillon's platforms caused speculation about the arrival of Thatcherite economics in France; yet what the two men proposed can be properly understood as Thatcherism only in the context of the French's historic horror of "Anglo-Saxon economics," since what both had in mind was plainly another form of *Colbertisme* that aligns as neatly with Trump's economic nationalism as Fillon's cultural nationalism and social conservatism agreed with the President-elect's. (François Fillon knew how to "seduce" the Catholic electorate, *Le Monde* noted dryly.)

Finally, Donald Trump's approach to Russia and Vladimir Putin was congruent with Fillon's. Fillon, a personal friend of Putin's, was clearly bent on establishing a working relationship with the Kremlin, as De Gaulle was in his presidential days. Across Europe, the rising populist right (including in France), more concerned with the migrant threat from Africa and the Middle East than with Russia's possible aggression across the eastern European frontier, was already aligning itself with Moscow's anti-progressive and nationalist policies, and Fillon was ready to accommodate it. "Mr. Fillon's warmth toward Mr. Putin," the *New York Times* observed, "is apparently heartfelt, and it predated this election. What changed is French voters, who increasingly desired hard-line policies and signs of strength they perceived Mr. Putin as representing." Since De Gaulle removed France's troops from NATO in 1966 the country had viewed the organization with a skepticism similar to Trump's. A poll conducted by Pew in 2015 found majorities in France, Germany, and Italy opposed to defending an eastern NATO ally in the event of invasion by Russia, treaty obligation or no. Since Putin's invation of Ukraine, all of that, of course, is changed.

The American globalist elite has done, is continuing to do, and will do in the future its damnedest to present Trump, in or out of office, to the United States and to the world, as a political anomaly, a peculiarly American freak like Huey Long or Father Coughlin, albeit a spectacularly successful one. In truth, Trump remains, following his electoral defeat in 2020, something far bigger than himself, and bigger even than that portion of America he represents and speaks for. Trumpism is part of a groundswell across the West—the United States and Europe—against what R.R. Reno has identified and Pope Francis understands intuitively as "the emerging global governing class [that] has not won the loyalty of the masses, including the middle class in the West...."

Three weeks after the election on November 8, the *New York Times* printed an article detailing the effects Trump's victory was already having on political systems, and governments, everywhere in the world. In the four years between then and his leaving office, Donald Trump "went around the world," despite his being the greatest threat to what the English scholar and writer Ralph Berry calls "a hugely powerful concord—we do not have to call it a conspiracy—whose mighty forces bend politicians to their will." A political novice with superb political instincts who nevertheless is not a political creature in the sense, say, that William Jefferson Clinton is, Trump has spent his brief political career confronting the dominant political, economic, and social forces in postmodern life. Aristotle defined *homo sapiens* as a political animal. While he may or may not have intended this as a compliment, it has been taken as such for nearly two and a half millennia, no matter that men remain at another level of their being dishonest and murderous animals as much inclined to irrationality as to rationality. While classical liberalism suffered from an excess of rationalism, advanced liberalism in the 21st century is fundamentally irrational—especially under pressure, when it succumbs to actual hysteria as it is doing today. Trump and his people have always taken the full brunt of this organized and collectively direct emotionalism, with which they coped while in office as well as any administration could have been expected to do. From January 20, 2017, until January 20, 2021, Trump and those closest to him suffered a political assault amounting to a species of psychological warfare to which none of his predecessors had been subjected, an assault designed to distract, demoralize, and weaken the administration. In its determination to break the President down, remove him from office, and cancel his initiatives, the left resorted to "exposing" and attacking the most ordinary and innocent of executive functions, including the Chief Executive's candid expression of his sentiments, preferences, and wishes to his appointed subordinates charged by him with executing his policies. John Durham, the special prosecutor appointed by Attorney General William Barr to investigate the origins of the charge of collusion between Trump's presidential campaign and the Kremlin, has recently shown that the Democratic Party and its allies in the media deliberately attempted to employ their own campaign of lies aimed at bringing down a duly elected sitting President. When one considers the extent and weight of the opposition arrayed against him, the fact that the President should have any solid accomplishments at all to his credit—and he has many to point to, out of office—is astonishing, as Susan Rice, Barack Obama's National Security Advisor, has admitted.

But Donald Trump's enduring importance is wider, deeper, and more generalized than any executive order, appointment, or legislative accomplishment suggests. His great achievement as President, one that cannot be nullified, erased, or otherwise taken from him, was to have altered forever the nature and grounds of political debate in America, the Western world, and by extension those other parts of it that for decades have looked to the United States and Western Europe for their inspiration and their model, their understanding of modernity, and its anticipated successor. Trump is indeed the boy standing in the street as the emperor passes by on parade, with this difference: the emperor is not naked, he's transgendered and in drag. Trump has successfully mocked, disdained, ridiculed, and heaped contempt upon the international left's most cherished idols and shibboleths, while encouraging the country and the world beyond it to join him in doing so. After Donald Trump, a multitude of liberal causes, obsessions, fantasies, fads, assumptions, prejudices, pieties, platitudes, and slogans will never look or sound the same again—bear the same sheen, or carry the same ring. Since Trump's announcement of his presidential candidacy on July 16, 2015, certain obvious truths about the human individual and human society that could not previously be expressed in "polite" society have forced themselves upon contemporary political discourse, ones liberals will no longer be able to censor, hide, or bury. Trump's demystification and desacralization of the tenets of advanced liberalism are the ultimate reason for the left's uncontrolled fury and uncontrolled hatred of the man. In its eyes this is by far the greatest offense he has committed: the liberal equivalent of the Sin Against the Holy Ghost that Christ taught is the sole unforgivable sin. Subsequent elections in France, the Netherlands, and Great Britain gave the governors of the European Union a false sense of security concerning what they dismiss as "populism," a movement they assert has crested, "for the time being." What European officials welcomed as a defeat for "populism" in the Low Countries in March 2017 was exactly the opposite, while Labour's close-run campaign in Britain's General Election three months later signaled the strength of left-wing "populists" as well as right-wing ones. The European Commission should have taken no reassurance from the unexpected "success" of Jeremy Corbyn in gaining Parliamentary seats in the general election on June 9, 2017; the man who (though he amended certain of his views within a few days after the election) had previously criticized the E.U. as undemocratic and an engine for transforming its smaller members into "colonies of debt peonage," called NATO "a danger to world peace," compared Israel to an Islamic state while supporting an economic boycott of that country, and promised that as Prime Minister he would refuse to retaliate against incoming nuclear warheads with Britain's nuclear arsenal. The unrepresentative bureaucrats in Brussels are welcome to their opinion, which in any case encourages them to let down their guard against their formidable "populist" opponents (assuming that they truly believe the comforting stories they tell themselves).

Lastly, it is owing to former President Trump that for the first time in more than century and a half America exerted, for four years, a global political influence conducive to the preservation of liberty and the pursuit of essential human things vastly superior to, and more rewarding than, the pursuit of money, power, a false and destructive notion of "freedom," and aggressive ideological fantasies that, were they ever realized, could end only in a tyranny supported by digital technology and manipulated by bland monsters endowed with an inhuman power of which history has never known the like.

3. 2020: A Counter-Rebellion That Wasn't

The election of 2020 that ousted Donald Trump from the White House was as remarkable as the one four years before it that had sent him there. The result was the rejection by a narrow margin of the messenger of the new realignment in American politics—but also, as the vigorous popular reaction against his successor's first two years in office has shown, the retention of the message. Liberal and progressive Democrats, ebullient in victory yet dismayed and appalled by Trump's addition of some 10 million votes to his total of 64 million in 2016, grasped the significance of this fact at once. Their response was to act as though they had won a mandate from the electorate to reverse every one of the preceding administration's policies and replace them with their hard-left opposites, partly in a spirit of revenge but chiefly because they were—they are— horribly aware that one-half of the country, if not slightly more, remains center-right at the very least. Aware, too, of the mental incompetency of their new man in the Oval Office and the fatal unlikability of his Vice-President, they understood that they had two years to set the nation on what they hoped would be an irreversible path toward the "transformation" they wish for in a perilous gamble against time. Their strategy, in fact, amounts to a *blitzkrieg* against their political enemy, calculated to destroy his troops and other political resources and lock their own policies into place before he can elect new recruits and launch an effective counter-attack. The political climate, they understand all too well, is shifting away from them; and if they are to prevail in the long run it must be by such undemocratic means as seizing control of the major institutions of government, nationalizing the electoral system and controlling that as well, packing the Supreme Court, replacing the American citizenry by grateful illegal aliens obedient to their will and eager for their patronage and material benefits, substituting a frankly socialist economy for an already mixed one, making the American public wholly dependent on Washington in their quotidian relationship with it, merging the federal government with a global bureaucratic one, weakening the nation-state as a conceptual as well as an actual reality, and treating Americans as though they were citizens of the world, not the United States, while ignoring all traditional distinctions between them—of sex,

11

race, ethnicity, class, wealth, intelligence, ability, talents, and so forth—that they cannot actually erase. It is an absurdly ambitious, even a mad, agenda, as well as one impossible to achieve; but the rationalist left, as a new religion, has always believed in miracles as it imagines them, and so it presses on: fervently, but in kind of desperate panic, knowing the deadly constraints of time and of fortune they have to contend with.

It may be, however, that Donald Trump, having broken the mold in which previous Republican presidential candidates were cast and thus shown the way toward Republican victories in future, has made too many enemies along the way (among "nice" Republicans, female ones especially) to prevail against a Democratic opponent in 2024. Should that be the case, the GOP will have—for the first time in a very long while—strong new talent to replace him with in the next quadrennial election. You can fool half a nation for a very long time, but the American people have historically been predominantly a gritty, obstinate, cross-grained, and irascible lot with a dislike of being fooled, lied to, cheated, and bilked. Modern liberalism has been doing all those things—and more—for many decades now, but for half of them, at least, the liberal illusionist show is no longer convincing, but threatening. Lincoln, were he living today, would feel his political instincts vindicated—in this respect, at least.

CHAPTER TWO | INCOHERENT LIBERALISM

Following Brexit in the summer of 2016 and Donald Trump's election five months later, liberals were widely said to deny the significance of these and subsequent events. Their first response to the British referendum and the American general election was that "the wrong people won" the two latest major political contests in the English-speaking world. We have since learned that they understood better than they admitted at the time the significance of these disruptions. President Obama has been quoted in a book by a senior aid as having wondered, immediately after the election, whether "we were wrong," and speculated that his presidency might have been ten to twenty years ahead of its time. The statement implies that he believes that, a decade or two on, the advanced liberalism he represents and tried to impose on the United States during his eight years in office will be politically acceptable to the American public and adapted to the political and social realities of the next generation. His reputation as an intellectual and an orator to the contrary, Obama is neither a reflective and widely read man nor an especially intelligent one, which explains his inability to recognize the intellectual and practical deficiencies of the contemporary liberal creed. Others see more clearly, as an article in *The Economist* (June 15 2018) suggested. "The global elites have reduced one of the world's richest philosophies [liberalism] to a dessicated husk of its former self." The quote is from Walter Bagehot, editor-in-chief of the liberal periodical *The Economist* in the mid 19th century. As the English scholar and critic Ralph Berry has remarked (in a private letter), "We are looking at the crisis in the liberal world order when a high priest of liberalism ascends the pulpit to deliver the weekly sermon, and it's the above quote, something very big is happening."

Here Bagehot's *portavoce* expressed a degree of self-awareness that is rare among the majority of liberal commentators who have put Trump's election down to demagoguery, nihilism, racism, and recent economic history. The first three of these are calumnious, but the fourth is both a facile excuse and a natural mistake on the part of people who believe in the primacy of economics in explaining history and human behavior. Other liberal commentators have concluded that, "We were wrong to put our faith in democracy," as Stephen Bush, a columnist for *The New Statesman* in England wrote, and that political consensus in European governments achieved through "anti-right maneuvering, though an effective short-term solution to the volatility of contemporary democracy, can end up making the underlying causes of the volatility worse." At the root of the liberals' problem is their conviction that liberal democracy—democracy run by liberals—is the only valid form for democracy to take, and their belief that liberal governments can somehow ignore indefinitely the claims of "illiberal" democrats, and survive. They miss the great paradox of modernity, which is that the liberal creed that was developed by and for that peculiar breed of modern people we call intellectuals is, as a system, intellectually confused, contradictory, and vulnerable on almost every point to the processes of rational scrutiny and investigation they think they have monopolized from the beginning.

1. Liberalism in the Headlights

The murder of five white police officers in Dallas on July 8, 2016, immediately following the fatal shootings of a black man in Louisiana and another in Minnesota, gave President Obama the opportunity to engage in still another of the flights of soaring *clichés* and wafting banalities for which his admirers celebrate him; Hillary Clinton the chance to demonstrate once again that she is a towering bore even to her own followers; and the national media to indulge in more of their countless exercises in determining what the public reaction to that event and similar ones should be, and convincing the American public that the media's response is the one it is experiencing spontaneously.

In Dallas the president spoke of the many families he had hugged following similar incidents during his seven and a half years in office and of the inadequacy of his own words in addressing the nation; of the need to "build bridges" to prevent people from "hardening their positions" and "drawing lines" as they "retreat to their respective corners"; and of politicians' responsibility to resist "grabbing attention" and "avoiding the

fallout." Obama counseled against a fear that "the center won't hold"—
an attitude he condemned as "despair," though he did concede that, "it's
as if the deepest fault lines of our democracy have suddenly been exposed,
perhaps even widened." Mrs. Clinton, speaking in Springfield, Illinois,
lectured her proximate audience and the country at large on gun violence,
economic inequality, and "overreliance" on the police in the attempt to
cure social ills. She quoted Lincoln's warning about "a house divided,"
exhorted white Americans to listen more closely to the complaints of
black ones, called for a "national conversation" on race, and wrapped up
her remarks with the promise that, "if we do the work, we will cease to
be divided." Both her address and the President's were speeches that anyone could have written, and that indeed anybody appears to have done.
Lastly, the media swanned around bowing their violins as they described
"a nation in mourning" swamped by "waves of grief," apparently oblivious
to the observable fact that the vast majority of Americans wondered ab-
sently why the flags on their local government buildings should be at
half mast again, a thing that happens every week or two these days on
average. Among those people who pay little or no attention to the news
and to politics, most seemed to feel contempt, disgust, and an impersonal
skepticism regarding the future of the United States rather than grief,
whether genuine or *ersatz*.

In the week following the Fourth of July the politicians and the
media were the institutional face of a mass, elephantine, continental (but
otherwise formless, pluralistic and multicultural), post-democratic, digitalized, impersonal, incoherent, and increasingly ungovernable society
whose calculated purpose in formally addressing the nation is not to give
it the truth it might or might not desire but to pacify it, mollify it, and
direct its response into officially predetermined and approved channels.
As these people and the institutions they staff are almost entirely dis-
connected from the people whom they claim to represent after having
been elected by them (or appointed by their elected representatives), the
natural result is rhetorical falsity, artificiality, banality, and ultimate fu-
tility: communication that communicates nothing apart from its phony
personal, folksy touches and whose sole aim is to create a type of false
consciousness among the public. The office of president was designed by
the Framers to be that of Chief Executive of the United States, not its

High Priest or Consoler in Chief—a conveniently disingenuous part for modern presidents to play when they are really aspiring to the role of American Mikado.

In his reference to "fault lines" Obama seemed to have meant racial divides, the divide between black and white in particular. But the situation is infinitely more complicated than that. America is not simply divided, she is fractured in a craze of spreading lines and hairlines that trace the boundaries of ideological, cultural, religious, ethnic, and racial rivalries and resentments. Only a few weeks after the shootings in Dallas, the *New York Times* reported that the recent attention given the killings of blacks by the police is encouraging Mexican and other Latin activists to try to appropriate some of it for themselves by demanding that the cameras—and the politicians—turn round now to face their way.

The country is reaping the burden of a history shaped since 1865 by liberal thought and liberal politics. First came the "re-union" of North and South—in reality, no re-union at all but the forcible union of the institutional components of two broadly dissimilar geographic, social, and political regions that from 1789 until 1865 were considered by the Founders and their descendants to be comprised of sovereign states linked in voluntary and equal compact with one another. National "union" at the cost of 618, 222 men was succeeded by decades of the unrestrained free enterprise (excepting the tariff) favored by economic liberalism and a century and a half of increasingly liberal jurisprudence, liberalizing religion, liberalizing education, liberal secular metaphysics (described by George Santayana in *Character & Opinion in the United States*, published in 1920), liberalizing psychology, sociology, and economics, and their practical applications, social engineering and the encouragement of mass immigration by increasingly unlike, incompatible, and unassimilable peoples resulting in multiculturalism, social confusion, resentment, chaos, and public violence. Contrary to what the politicians promise, no political solution is possible for America's contemporary "problems," better described as "conditions." (James Burnham, the political philosopher, was fond of observing that, "Where there's no solution, there's no problem.") What used to be called the art of politics has long since become the abuse of it; while the most skillful government, unable to override or cancel history, is incapable of "solving," or even adequately coping with, troubles of the fundamentally nonpolitical sort—what the country is experiencing today along with all the Western democracies. As the US grapples ineffectually with racially motivated violence, the European countries struggle helplessly to combat terrorist attacks by citizens as well as foreign enemies. On both sides of the Atlantic—in Washington and Paris, in Berlin and Brussels—governments are paralyzed by their inability to devise solutions to their respective crises that are compatible with the scruples of the liberal creed and the liberal agenda that have given form and meaning to their national projects for two centuries. An efficient solution for racial strife and terrorism on the present scale could only be an illiberal one, and liberal governments (and the media) know this. Liberalism is no longer capable of controlling liberally the liberal society for which it is responsible, and so far it appears that liberals would prefer to see their liberal world destroyed by barbarians, foreign and domestic, than rescue it by illiberal means.

Science, the social "sciences," technology and technocracy, and universal affluence have encouraged modern people to imagine that humanity has conquered what used to be called "the human condition," and that every perceived social, economic, and political "problem" is now remedial by one technique or another, or simply by a sufficient sum of money thrown at it. But societies, like biological bodies, are ultimately self-healing, though artificial treatments may be devised to assist and promote the natural process. And though what we call "society" is a "body" only in the metaphorical sense, an organically malfunctioning society too must heal itself by the social equivalent of natural, organic means. The opportunistic and racially exploitive liberal politicians, the sensationalist, leftwing, anti-white mediacrats, and the Marxist multicultural academy who have implicitly sanctioned and encouraged racially aggressive organizations like Black Lives Matter and La Raza—the agents significantly responsible for the Western disease—are constitutionally incapable of curing it, even if they wished to. They can only aggravate the illness and its symptoms, as they are busily and enthusiastically doing in the face of social and political catastrophe. Healthy social and moral responses (beginning with religious ones) can only arise naturally, spontaneously, and even unconsciously, often without direct aim or seeming purpose; though a society reconstituted after liberalism's demise will likely bear little resemblance to its predecessor, even supposing it escaped the tyranny that historically has followed the collapse of democratic regimes. In any event, and under whatever form of government, racial antagonism in the United States and elsewhere is certain to persist in greater or lesser degree as the intractable problem it is today, and always has been, in racially mixed societies. Liberalism's vision of a post-racial society is a cruel, illusory, futile, and ultimately destructive dream, and a nation that cannot reconcile itself with reality can end only by driving itself mad, as America has been doing for decades now. Yet the alternative to post-racial politics is not white (or black, or brown) "identitarian" politics, it is post-utopian politics—or, in the context of the present era, post-liberal politics.

Liberal thought and the liberal agenda as it has evolved over the past two or three centuries are as exhausted in the 21st century as the liberal societies it created are. That is why liberalism today is showing its conservative aspect: its intellectual and dispositional rigidity and illiberalism and its intolerant ambition to prevail by imposing its formless irrational creed everywhere. Liberalism, and liberals, never give up. But liberalism, confronted by the insuperable ideological contradictions of a world of its own creation, has run out of the ideas necessary to maintain the liberal world. Its intellectual exhaustion is becoming obvious to more and more people in the West, and beyond it. As the modern *Ancien Régime*, the liberal Establishment finds itself the enemy of a new Third Estate that has not been served, but blocked and oppressed, by it. Liberals have nothing to say to these people, deriding them as ignorant "populists" motivated by class resentment, ignorance, and racial hatred. Liberals refuse to recognize that the new Western democratic movements, motivated by exploitive economies and transformative immigration policies, resent above everything liberalism's refusal ever to let up in its efforts to realize a more and more perfect society—and to let up on the people whom they must reform and dragoon in order to get there by forcing them into unnatural and inhuman pathways. No society can ever prevent or eradicate every social and political evil or imperfection; each needs to decide for itself which of these ills it should be prepared to accept as being simply a part of the human condition, and which not. But that is a decision liberals, and liberalism, are intellectually and temperamentally incapable of making, especially in regard to the matter of race, which has become their paramount—indeed, their beloved—obsession.

2. What Do Liberals Want?

The agenda of the Democratic Party, of liberal politicians generally—including socialist-liberals like Bernie Sanders and Keith Ellison—and of liberal academics and intellectuals, is embodied in the record of Barack Obama's two administrations and of Hillary Clinton's campaign, which ran on that record. Not nearly so clear is what the demonstrators who protested *en masse* in the streets against President Trump after his inauguration really wanted. Certain reporters who covered the demonstrations in Washington on January 20, 2017, and interviewed random participants noted that many seemed not to know themselves, beyond abortion on demand and free contraception for women. One young man, asked by a reporter why he was protesting that afternoon, replied with the wild-eyed look of a panicked actor who has forgotten his next lines: "Uh….my life is in danger!" As the weeks passed, the protestors' message gradually crystallized into one single-word exhortation: "Resist!" But resist *what*, exactly?

Uncertain as anyone, the *New York Times* dispatched a reporter to make inquiries, mainly among young or youngish people. When asked what "resist" meant, a young black woman replied "creating a society where we divest from things that punish and invest in real community-based measures that keep us safe." A female anti-First Amendment activist in her mid-30s said "resist" meant to get rid of "a variety of things that all make people uncomfortable and not able to rest well and feel like what they are doing is OK." A self-described "political and arts consultant" in Charlotte answered, "to stand up for the people who already make America great. The United States is diverse because we are a country of immigrants…." A young former press secretary for Senator Sanders' campaign defined "resistance" as "stand[ing] up for what we know is right and true, not because it's popular but because it is necessary." For a young rabbi, it meant "resisting the temptation to assume, to decide who is a person before spending time with him or her…. And more than anything, resist the easiness of just being angry—dig down past that anger, toward the pain." And a former male organizer, aged 25, for Mrs. Clinton said, "We have worked hard to get to where we are, and it's a little scary that we could move backward in the next two or four years. So to me it's making sure we are protecting what we have gained and pushing the envelope further and working to engage more people in the process." Tellingly, this atypically concrete explanation was offered by someone who had been directly involved in promoting the Obama-Clinton program that had just been superseded by that of the man liberals of all sorts never imagined could win the election. They rather assumed after eight years of "*Sí, si puedo!*" that the progressive assault on America had become unstoppable.

Obviously, none of this reflects anything that could credibly be described as a political movement based on reasoned political thinking as an expression of a political theory, or even as what today is inaccurately called "ideology." Anti-Trumpism in particular, like all popular leftism in its present form, is about feeling rather than thinking, self-expression in place of political understanding. For modern popular leftists, liberals, and progressives, government is more than a public institution, politics more than "the public thing." Government is not just outside them, asking certain things and giving others. It has become for these people essentially the private thing, something with an interior more than an exterior dimension, instead of the old *res publica*. The French writer Hervé Juvin, in his book *Le Gouvernement du Désir*, argues that consumer capitalism, having commodified the natural and the human worlds, now functions with "the government of desire" to mutually beneficial ends, each stimulating the desire for ever new, and always more, material and political goods. Taking Juvin's thesis a step further, one sees that the government of desire is not only about consumerism, profit, political power, and government itself: The phenomenon has psychological and even metaphysical elements as well. As R.R. Reno suggested in reference to "the democratic revolution that defines the modern era," this is a revolution "more of the imagination than of the mechanics of government"— or, one might add, its form. This explains why the left today seems to want a society that is at once collectivist *and* individualistic. The political left outside the Democratic Party seems through with liberalism, disillusioned by it, unable to feel intellectually or emotionally connected with it, yet unable to imagine any clear alternative. (President Obama wasn't really left enough for the left, though leftists were willing enough to support his presidency as a way station on the journey they wished to take.) Hence their angry, vengeful, pseudo-revolutionary frustration. Nietzsche's Last Man has arrived in the very modern form of a mass movement, and he is living in a mental vacuum and emotional agony. For several decades now, young people have been taught not to think except in the most instrumental ways and under the direction of their ideologically exacting liberal teachers; never in a manner that might allow them to rediscover traditional philosophical and political solutions, or even the means by which to approach them. Indeed, they have not been taught what is real or true at all, rather the opposite. So the left cannot satisfactorily imagine a post-liberal future, as the right can only imagine a return to the classical liberal past.

This is a cause of the political situation today, when a blind and angry super-partisanship virtually guarantees that even the smallest political incident or scandal (like General Flynn's pre-inaugural conversations with Russian officials) becomes a political crisis. Modern, advanced liberalism—which is a kind of demagoguery of and by the educated and upper classes, as in certain of its previous forms it was demagoguery of and by the lower and uneducated ones—is responsible for this. With the presidency of Donald Trump, reality hit unreality, as matter smashes violently into anti-matter. Finally, modern women—and many modern men of the metro-sexual sort—simply could not cope, mentally and emotionally, with a traditionally aggressive male in the White House. It was partly a matter of types and stereotypes. Liberals have them, too.

The question of secession is supposed to have been settled over a century and a half ago by Abraham Lincoln. But now one liberal state is openly threatening to secede from the Union, and others are making more discreet sounds in favor of going the same road. We shall see what, if anything, comes of this. Meanwhile, the inverse possibility has never been raised, or even imagined. Can the federal government *expel* a state? It is perhaps a question for the current Democratic administration to consider. Like Titipu's Lord High Executioner, many people are probably keeping "a little list." Again, we shall see....

For the present, advanced liberalism continues to function as an instinctive unreasoning force, a sea eroding a continental civilization on its eastern and western sides.

3. Humanity-Lite

Since the Sixties liberals have talked about "victimless crimes," offenses that are prosecutable by law but that liberals claim "hurt no one." Prominent among these were homosexual encounters, consenting or not, which over the next several decades were decriminalized by most states and eventually recognized by the U.S. Supreme Court as acts of love, and finally conjugal love, harmless to society and actually beneficial to it. (How can there be too much love in the world?) Yet the liberal premise is false. Homosexual "marriage" is not simply a contradiction in terms; it is a form of moral and logical insanity that is harmful to everyone in society, liberals and homosexuals included. As Gloucester says in *King Lear*: "'Tis the times' plague, when madmen lead the blind."

The world is infinitely more complex than liberals imagine, but the little of it they do recognize—like the institution of marriage—they complicate absurdly. Marriage is one of those very basic and simple things one would think the human race wouldn't need to be arguing about after so many millennia. But liberals have made it into an issue as controversial as climate change, without perceiving that gay "marriage" is more perilous to the human race than global warming is. A practical knowledge of nature is useful to men but a proper knowledge of man is absolutely crucial. And liberalism has avoided self-understanding (distinguished from psychiatry) from the beginning.

The world liberalism made is comparable to a child's terrarium set down in a vast wilderness beneath a starry sky, to which its pet inhabitants are blind and whose existence they do not even suspect. The difference is that the child—the inventor of this small, narrow, incomplete, sealed off, make-believe world—lives in the tank together with the creatures he manages. In order to make himself great, the liberal has made himself small. In attempting to free himself, he has put himself into prison. Thinking he is reinventing himself, he imagines he is a simpler being than a painted turtle, and he is trying to do the same with the world he is determined to remake according to his vision of the ideal one. He boasts of the dignity of man, and unconsciously denies it by denying that man has a nature—the sole ground of his dignity—at all. The liberal is like the robot who recently killed his German handler except that he isn't a robot, he only thinks he's one; crazy as the man who is convinced he's really a bed-bug. Liberal humanism, the doctrine of the self-sufficiency and the supremacy of man, is the self-imagined robot's owner's manual, written by himself.

Justice Kennedy based his decision in *Obergerfell v. Hodges* principally on his affirmation of an equal human dignity possessed by all men and women. But the dignity of human beings is something liberals refute even as they assert it. Liberals who believe in God, or think or say they do, would likely agree that the dignity of God is attributable partly to his immutable nature, to his being above and beyond the universal flux. Mortal men are not changeless but the immutability of their nature is something they share with God, on Earth as in Heaven. Would the dignity of God be enhanced, or compromised, could He turn Himself into a turtle bearing the world on His back? Would Man's dignity be either could he change himself into Woman—or Robot, as the Transhumanists confidently expect to do?

Advanced liberalism exalts Man above all things, believing there is nothing in the universe higher than Man. But liberalism, which for centuries has accused conservatism—and Christianity—of holding an allegedly dark and pessimistic view of human nature, is far more distrustful of humanity than either of the others is. That is why liberals wish to manipulate and massage it for the purpose of perfecting it.

Liberalism's quarrel with humanity is not that it is insufficiently human but just the opposite, " it is human, all too human": too sunk in the state of nature, too physical, too active, too aggressive, too selfish and materialistic, too excitable, emotional, and irrational, too credulous, timorous, and prone to religious superstition, too willful and wayward and rebellious, *too vital* and *too real*—above all, too swinishly resigned to being itself and too resistant to the program of redemption by liberalism. Liberals like humanity the way they like their beer, with as few calories as possible. Their ideal is Humanity-Lite, which explains the ubiquity today of the metro-sexual male and his un-sexed female counterpart in the professions, the universities, and the bureaucracy, culture remaking itself in their image. It further explains liberal resistance to metaphysics and traditional religion, which liberals have replaced to their own satisfaction with a Faith-Lite substitute for Christianity—a Religion Without Religion that takes Hazel Motes's Church of Christ Without Christ a few steps further down the road to outright unbelief and metaphysical rebellion. "We shall not serve."

Liberals love to speak about "identity" and are constantly discovering and asserting new identities everywhere, but they grow uncomfortable when assertion passes beyond navel-gazing and festive and colorful street demonstrations. Liberalism encourages what it calls diversity, but what it is really after is sameness under the skin—still more under the cranium. (Diversity for liberals is usually only skin deep, which seems odd for people who see racism everywhere while insisting that race is a "social construction." The discrepancy can probably be explained by modern liberalism's hidden premise that some races are more equal that others.) Evelyn Waugh dismissed the 20th century as the Century of the Common Man. Liberals, unsatisfied by that democratic triumph, propose to make the 21st century the Century of the Commonness of Man, dominated and managed and manipulated by the uncommon elite that dares not speak its name and prefers to keep its superior self out of sight in gated communities when it is not running for political office.

Liberals, indignantly rejecting the age-old wisdom that "boys will be boys," are determined to prove the adage false in the schools. The maxim is "sexist," for one thing. For another, normal, healthy male behavior, juvenile or adult, is deeply offensive to feminists, educators, and later in life to company managers, owing to its primitive physicality, self-assertive exuberance, and because it disrupts their scientifically structured environments. (Female nature is far more compatible with liberal preferences and assumptions—liberalism since the Great War has been increasingly feminized in persuasion and in practice—but only so long as everyone agrees that there really is no such thing.) The unquestionable liberal assumption that every girl can—and should—grow up to play whatever role she wishes to in the world, including those of the soldier and the police officer, which are distrusted by liberals when they are played by males, comports with liberals' ideological belief in the absolute interchangeability of all people in every human activity; this includes sexual intercourse, and the certainty that anybody can be whatever he chooses to be, provided he is given the resources to which he has a human right and nobody stands in his way. Sexual identity, like racial identity, previously in the eye of the beholder, now resides in the mind of the beheld. The days of the *Moulin Rouge* are over, and *"Vive la différence!"* as an acceptable liberal sentiment is long gone.

The sole identity liberalism is willing to recognize is religious identity, though even here the acknowledgment is blurred by the confident liberal conviction that either all gods are one and the same, or that "There is No God but No God"—no supernatural world behind the painted backdrop, no Heaven, no Hell, no angels, no demons, nothing but seven billion-plus bipeds wandering aimlessly across the surface of a ball of mud and rock circling a sphere of flaming gasses. Eliot said that human beings cannot bear too much truth. It seems equally obvious that they cannot bear too much happiness either, if they happen to be of the liberal persuasion especially. Perhaps this is why the affluent West, driven by liberalism, is abandoning the Christian faith that formed and sustained it for two thousand years. In any event, one distinction modern liberals can be counted on to draw between one religion and another is the basic distinction in their minds: bad, badder, badder still, worst, and absolute worst.

As the heavens proclaim the greatness of the Lord, politics, society, and the news media tell the madness (the irrational rationality) of the modern West hour by hour, minute by minute. So, more significantly, does the art world as we have known it for the last seven decades.

Despite the relatively few genuine artistic accomplishments of the post-war era, and some truly great artistic careers that have spanned them, Western art—music, literature, architecture, painting and sculpture, philosophy—has been something less than the Sahara of the Bozart. It has been, rather, the Bozart of the Sahara: a Sahara of fraud, dishonesty, lies, incompetence, ignorance, vulgarity, egotism, celebrity seeking, greed, stupidity, and blasphemy. The reasons for the disaster are many, but behind them all is One Big Reason: the fatally impoverished liberal cosmology and anthropology, operating together like a giant pump to suck the oxygen out of a living and breathing world to make way for the displacement of its vibrant creatures by two dimensional forms and shadows motivated by abstractions as illusory as they are themselves.

There have been periods in history, marked by social and political turmoil and warfare, when the arts and learning continued to flourish and sometimes, as in the Renaissance, even surpassed their previous achievements. Another example is the interwar period, 1918–39, the golden age of Modernism in literature especially. The early 21ˢᵗ century, though equally one of global chaos, is not such a time, and for this the anti-culture of advanced liberalism is responsible. The certain grip on reality that high culture—any culture worthy of the name—requires depends directly upon its mental and moral sanity rooted in an intellectually coherent religious tradition that shapes and colors it, while explaining to men what man truly is.

Here are two texts that profoundly express the soul of the Christian religion. The first is from St. Paul's "Letter to the Romans": "…I have in my heart a great sorrow and continual suffering" (9:1). The second is part of a prayer written by the 20ᵗʰ century Italian priest David Maria Turoldo: "Lord, thank you for the day and for the night, for what we understand and for what we do not understand; thank you for good and for evil, for what you give and for what you take away; thank you for life and for death; but above all, thank you for the resurrection of your Son, and ours.…" No modern liberal could have written these lines by Paul and Turoldo, or anything like them—because he couldn't imagine a rational man entertaining such "irrational" thoughts as theirs.

Liberalism *truimphans* cannot understand how anyone could possibly choose to experience a lifetime of perpetual sorrow and mental suffering, let alone hold them close to his heart. Nor can it imagine thanking God for withholding understanding of any kind from His people; for permitting the existence of evil in the world; for withdrawing His benefits after having granted them; for sending them death; and for encouraging superstitious myths like the Resurrection among them. Liberalism, unable to recognize that tragedy is an essential part of the nature of man, has replaced it with a shallow triumphalism; the struggle between good and evil with endless "progress"; an appreciation of sorrow and suffering with medications for the mind and the body; the conception of physical death as the beginning of a new life with nihilistic despair or helpless resignation. Robert Frost said that there is no poetry in money. If such a thing is possible, there is even less poetry in the liberal

view of the universe. (Shakespeare, for one, knew how to make great poetry out of men's *lust* for gold.)

By their arts you may know them....Turoldo's prayer deserves to be
called the artist's prayer, and its total incompatibility with the modern
spirit goes a long way toward explaining why there are so few artists—
though are innumerable officially acclaimed "Artists" and "Geniuses"—
in our time, which refuses to recognize the metaphysical grounding that
is the absolute *fons et origen* of all art. The result is a culture, thinner than
blue milk, that has surrendered and subordinated itself to mass politics,
leftist social causes, progressivism, and propaganda—scarcely superior,
if superior at all, to the Soviet culture of the 30s and 40s, and similarly
detached from reality. Today, the term "artist" is frequently as much a
misnomer as is the word "spouse" applied to the partners in a homosexual
"marriage."

4. Suffering without God

*"If other ages felt less, they saw more, even though they saw with the
blind, prophetical, unsentimental eye of acceptance, which is to say, of faith."*
—Flannery O'Connor

Patricia Snow cites the sentence above, taken from O'Connor's introduction to *A Memoir of Mary Ann*, in a brilliant essay in *First Things*
("Empathy Is Not Charity," October, 2017). "A lot has happened in three
hundred years," Snow writes. "As secularization has advanced and man
has had to learn to live without God, his solution for the most part has
been to draw closer to other people, in unprecedented, ultimately unten-
able ways." The "death of God" thesis causes people to consider what we
owe to other people in a world in which only human beings can help
themselves, and others. In a God-forsaken universe, sharing others' sufferings (though much less their joys) becomes a moral obligation in an "age
of empathy" (in the Dutch primatogist's Frans de Waal's phrase), an age
not of reason but of unconstrained emotion. "Is it a coincidence," Snow
asks, "that in a world that has made a fetish of vicarious suffering, suffering itself—real suffering—has become taboo?" Modern man's—liberal
man's—imagined imperative duty is to discover suffering wherever it

exists in the world, and to eradicate it. A Christian objection to this imperative is that suffering is not an absolute evil, like sin—it is suffering that brings us closest to God. Among Patricia Snow's concerns is that "in a world without God, man attributes too much agency to himself." Another comes from her perception that "Empathy solidarity…is Christian solidarity's demonic counterfeit, one that carries within itself the seeds of its own destruction. If the Holy Spirit strengthens both individuals and the ties that bind them, empathy weakens them. Excessive, unmediated intimacy leads to affective confusion (whose suffering is whose?), and even to confusion about identity and agency (whose choices are whose?)." She concludes, "Our culturally sanctioned practice of empathy is an attempt to fill Christ's shoes; it is a reiteration of the sin of Eden in a fresh guise. In place of Christ's fearless, definitive Passion, we offer others our problematic, uneasy pity, a passion from which no one rises incorrupt."

Patricia Snow's insight points in two directions. One is to what is best and most noble in the human spirit, especially perhaps when that spirit is most naive. The other is toward liberalism at its most false, most dishonest, most self-serving, and most manipulative, and the effect it has had in shaping the modern liberal world for the worse in spite of the fact that, as Snow reminds us, people today are no more selfish and egotistical than they ever were.

Liberalism has worked for three centuries toward reshaping the world to its own deliberate ends by creating an imaginary alternative one, and, since 1789, toward creating a new people to realize that world and populate it. Understanding that the way to achieve their ambition is for the liberal avant-garde in politics, commerce, society, culture, and the arts to encourage people to think—and, especially, to *feel*—as liberals think and feel, liberals since the French Revolution have concentrated on constructing an intellectual and emotional context conducive the liberal project. Since the liberal view of human nature is wishful and unnatural, liberals have needed to be almost preternaturally inventive in devising ways to establish that context. These have included developing a new political philosophy that in fact is not philosophical at all (the ancients would have recognized this at once), denying the existence of God and persecuting the Church and the churches, "discovering" what does not exist (the "Brotherhood of Man") and what never could exist (perfect liberty and the universal equality of men), butchering members of the *Ancien Régime* while not overlooking apparent details like starting the calendar over again and renaming the months of the year to reflect the new revolutionary culture.

The early liberal era (most of the 19th century), itself sanguinary enough, was followed in the 20th by mass extermination on an industrial scale by totalitarian movements for which liberals always deny philosophical responsibility, though both communism and fascism obviously had their intellectual roots in the bloody liberal utopianism of 1789. Since the defeat of fascism in 1945 and the collapse of communism in 1991, mainstream liberals, while simultaneously waging brutally destructive and seemingly endless wars to impose modern liberal democracy on the world, have emphasized the empathetic, educational, and therapeutic aspects of liberalism over the militant ones, waging metaphorical wars globally against poverty, funding plans for global economic development, promoting the rights of women, children, and minorities everywhere, working to abolish international borders to facilitate the free movements of peoples, and to eradicate (by stealth) the Christian religion everywhere. From the end of World War II until 1991, American hegemony was chiefly supported and extended by America's "hard" power—the State Department and the Pentagon—despite "soft" programs like the Marshall Plan, critical support for the United Nations, the Peace Corps, and so on.

Since then, though, despite Washington's aggressive ideological wars to establish and support what it claims are democratic regimes, the liberalism embodied by "the indispensable nation" and her allies has been less the work of the Pentagon and Foggy Bottom and much more of America's liberal educational system, various and well funded international "centers" and "institutes" for the care and feeding of democracy, the liberal media, liberal Hollywood and the artistic world generally, Madison Avenue, and Wall Street. For the past quarter-century advanced liberalism has relied on an illusory world conjured by relentlessly ideological education, biased news reporting and commentary, psychological manipulation, and moral intimidation, all made plausible and possible by weakened Christianity, distorted and misrepresented equally by liberal "Christians" and secular liberals. A psychological sleight-of-hand has been practiced all along, a trick that liberals themselves, when they think they think they see it being worked by the conservative enemy, call brain-washing. There is nothing new here: In the good old days of not-so-advanced liberalism, liberals invoked "democracy" rather than "the global community," "freedom" instead of "rights," "free enterprise" for "economic fairness," and so forth. It is all a matter of what are called God terms: words that carry instant authority simply by being spoken, and command unthinking respect merely from being heard. Advanced liberalism too relies on many God terms, among which none is more sacrosanct than "compassion," and the "empathy" so effectively scrutinized by Patricia Snow.

She thinks that today's observable obsession with individuality indicates rather "a deficit rather than a surfeit." In a world without God, people no longer know "where they end and where they begin." The sense of individuality they guard so fiercely is actually weak and uncertain. But Christianity can only flourish or be passed forward by strong individuals endowed with a sense of an integral self. Christianity is a religion that accepts for a fact that Everyman has it in him to lead a heroic life which is what the Christian life, truly and faithfully lived, is. As a Christian herself, Snow's primary concern is for the person of today, "[s]uspicious of others' influence and terrified of exercising his own, frightened of suffering himself but even more unnerved by the thought of others suffering—how can such a person receive Christ or offer [H]im to others, when either to receive or propose Christ is always, at the same time, to receive and propose [H]is cross [sic]? In a suffering-averse world, handing on the Gospel is almost impossible." She is absolutely right, of course. Yet (and I imagine she knows this) the corrosive effects of liberalism's insistence that "compassion" and "empathy" are human obligations with a universal reach extend well beyond her particular concern.

The Church has always taught that our primary charitable obligation is to those nearest us—those with whom our relationship is a personal one. Charity is a personal and particular—a very *real*—thing which, in being universalized, loses both its personal and its human reality. It is made an abstraction which, insofar as it has any reality at all, is merely a form of generalized benevolence which, like philanthropy, is not charity itself. (It is no coincidence that an age in which every sort of personal immorality is rampant, accepted, and even celebrated has been ironically described as an "age of conspicuous benevolence.") The same goes for empathy, since, while the need for personal charity is present and obvious, the causes of universal suffering can only be imagined, and imagined badly—incompletely, or not at all. Human beings are as incapable of feeling for the entire world as they are of knowing it (partly *because* they cannot know it), though they may easily fool themselves into thinking— or "feeling"—that they do, usually for egotistical or dishonest reasons. This is true especially of Christians, whose religion is a deeply personal one based on the revealed fact of divine sonship. True empathy is the re- sult of an immediate confrontation with suffering that permits direct personal acts to alleviate both the suffering *and* the empathy, which has now been deprived its object, its cause.

The affirmed obligation to experience universal empathy is a cruel, self-serving trick of liberalism, which, beyond inducing unwarranted sen- timents of personal guilt, encourages people not toward charitable love but instead a sense of impotence to perform effective acts of mercy, chill- ing and hardening the heart while leaving it burdened with an equally strong conviction of guilt. In a time of universal benevolence that is also an age of instant global communication ceaselessly transmitting news of humanitarian horrors and all sorts of suffering situations—news, liberals insist, that we have an ancillary charitable obligation to follow consci- entiously—liberalism's insistence on universal empathy registered in- stantly, automatically, and unreflectively as a moral obligation is as self-defeating as it is inhumane, unreasonable, and unrealistic. Impotence in the face of suffering eventually prompts decent and humane people to respond cynically and callously to suffering at a distance, especially when they recognize that they are being relentlessly manipulated by the politicians, the media, and the global relief and "charitable" organizations to feel things they are humanly incapable of feeling in the circumstances, and acquaint themselves with suffering situations they cannot compre- hend or relieve. A profoundly human and altogether excusable response to still another massacre of its people by some African government, or a mass human stampede killing hundreds in India after a train breaks down at a railway station, or brutal civil war in Yemen, or rape, warfare, and starvation in Sudan is carelessly to dismiss the disaster: "Oh, that's just the way those people are." (A response by a character in one of Waugh's novels to the outbreak of riots in Northeast Africa—"Just a bunch of niggers having a revolution"—struck nobody eighty years ago as anything other than humanly recognizable, and thus amusing.)

The universalization of "compassion" and "empathy" is just one of innumerable attempts by liberal persons, classes, parties, private organizations, and governments to alter human behavior and redesign human nature by a sort of forced Lamarckian process. The predictable result is the same old impervious humanity, pressed by ambitious and power-hungry cynics to imagine that they experience sentiments of dishonest mercy, false justice, and imagined sympathy when informed of remote sufferings easily exploitable by calculating liberals, who, more than anyone else, stand to benefit from a shallow "empathetic" response to them on a mass public scale.

5. "Only What Is Not Is Beautiful"

Tocqueville was the first author to apply the adjective "exceptional" to America, but the compliment—if he meant it as a compliment—was a backhanded one, a narrow reference to circumstances that "concurred to fix the mind of the American upon purely practical pursuits." Certainly he had nothing in mind comparable to the notion of "American exceptionalism" that formed in the 1920s, the smug, self-congratulatory postwar decade pride in the nation that had saved the world for democracy and made Jay Gatz stinking rich. Other countries have thought themselves "special" in some way, even simply "the best," but that is something else again. Imagine a brash youth in more or less polite society button-holing all who will listen to explain that he is an exceptional person, gifted with exceptional moral qualities and practical abilities and entitled to special consideration of his views and enterprises. Like most such young men (they are a proliferating breed nowadays) this one, upon closer consideration, would likely be found quite an ordinary fellow. The same goes for America. America is exceptional only in the sense that she considers herself exceptional, and shamelessly expresses that self-assessment in public.

Supposing America really *were* an exceptional nation, her constitutive parts would be exceptional too, starting with her public men and women.

32

An exceptional country would be ruled by statesmen, not merely the better sort of politician, not to mention some of the worst. But America is virtually devoid of statesmen; and the politicians that swarm in her capital cities and across her broad and fruitful lands, sea to shining sea, are plainly no better than those of the other civilized democracies. While the causes of the progressive destruction of America are many, the degraded American political class is the largest and most obvious one.

Still, American politicians are not the American people. Surely *they* are the best on earth—the most idealistic, the most enlightened, the most progressive, the most dynamic, the most religious, the most wholesome, the most *decent*. Yet it is they who elect the politicians. Certainly democratic politicos can be very cunning, very persuasive, very believable, as full of lies and trickery as a liberal theologian. But surely also an exceptional people should easily see through the virtual finery and the cosmetic surgery to the naked flabby flesh underneath.

And America has grown measurably less exceptional over the past three-quarters of a century—what used to be called the American century—as her industrial economy has weakened, her social structural decayed, her educational system collapsed, and her military failed in every war it embarked on from 1945 down to the present strategy to "degrade" the Islamic State, which it almost certainly cannot eradicate altogether. Americans' success at subduing and developing a continent and creating fabulous wealth in the process encouraged them to imagine themselves capable of succeeding spectacularly at any task they might decide to put their hand to. In reality, Americans since the Founding generation have shown as much inattentiveness as enthusiasm to matters of state, partly from lack of interest in history and what were once called general ideas, but also because their preoccupation with "practical objects" encouraged them to ignore philosophy as substantial intellectual debate and concentrate instead on the combative sporting element of party politics. (Sir Henry Maine made the same complaint about the democratic British electorate in the second half of the 19th century, when he observed that the contest between the Liberal and Tory parties had devolved into "a never-ending cricket match between Blue and Yellow.")

Americans have typically been indifferent to nearly everything that is not American, or American inspired, or in imitation of America. This indifference has allowed American diplomats to ignore their first responsibility, which is to advance the national interests of the United States in the world, and instead to promote the global financial interests of their wealthiest backers and the ideological obsessions of their academic and intellectual supporters by signing up to international free-trade agreements, facilitating the arrival of scores of millions of Third World immigrants and "refugees" in the "homeland," catering to the ethnic and nationalist loyalties of poorly-assimilated immigrants, clearing the ground upon which the White House plans to erect new liberal-democratic states out of the Mesopotamian sands and the jungles of Africa, reeducating the world according to the Gospel of Leo Strauss, and pluming their credentialed egos.

The principal things foreign governments look to the United States in the 21st century for are more money and an ally willing to bear the brunt of the dangerous and costly work Western governments insist needs to be done in places like Iraq, Afghanistan, and Ukraine. The achievement of "exceptional" diplomacy has replaced prudent self-interest and *realpolitik* with other-directed policies and liberal ideology as the mainstay of Western diplomacy. While this may be exceptionalism of some sort, it is not the kind that promotes the strength and survival of any nation, exceptional or otherwise. America has paid a huge price over the last century for her self-indulgent embrace of the exceptionalist myth, and she will pay still more in future.

The concept of American exceptionalism is both an elitist and a popular one. The Founders believed they were creating something new in political history, even perhaps something special, but a claim of "exceptionalism" would surely have caught in their throats. Sophisticated and highly educated gentlemen, men intellectually of the Old World accepting command of the New one, they did not live in a soap bubble. Many of their constituents, however, did. And as American democracy in the 19th century became more democratic (a process of "democratizing democracy," as someone has said), better developed economically, and much wealthier, Americans (like Mark Twain traveling in Europe) grew increasingly conscious of their imagined superiority in comparison with the peoples of the Old World and its customs. This attitude was naturally perpetuated by the "exceptional politicians" they elected from among themselves. Also, a tendency in American Protestant thought from its Puritan beginnings in New England—one easily misinterpreted by uneducated people as putting narrow morality above broad intellect—helped make exceptionalism appealing to the ignorant by encouraging a moralistic demeanor, suspicious of intellectual rigor, during the Great Awakening and in the early decades of the new democratic Republic.

The United States enjoyed the invaluable double advantage, as Tocqueville noted, of her geographical isolation from the parent civilization and her European cultural and religious heritage—the best of two worlds. At her back, stretching westward (after the Louisiana Purchase in 1803) to the Pacific Ocean, lay a continent equal to her ambitions: a three million square mile quarry containing the finest virgin marble and awaiting exploitation and development by scores of millions of future Michelangelos and Berninis, titans of frontier agriculture, finance, commerce, and industry, nothing and no one to oppose them but scattered fistfuls of the native Bronze Age tribes. The second advantage was political: The new republic played a major role in a dynamic revolutionary age that promised an expansion of political and social freedoms as limitless as the continent itself. Still a third, unmentioned by Tocqueville who arrived in America almost before the fact, was economic. The year eighteen-hundred, eleven years after Washington's First Inauguration, is the date commonly indentified by historians as the beginning of the Industrial Revolution, whose benefits the United States enjoyed during the first two-thirds of the 19th century while suffering relatively few of what economists call its "externalities" by comparison with Great Britain, France, and Germany. Her good fortune was related to America's youth, her economic and social flexibility, and her geographic space, which prevented severe over-crowding in the new industrial cities and offset the new industrial wastelands by vast tracts of agricultural land and virgin wilderness, allowing her industrial capacity and national wealth to grew at so great a pace that by the end of the century they rivaled Britain's, at the cost of perhaps half or less the social misery. In 1789 Americans set out to create a thriving modern democracy—admirable in many ways, but hardly exceptional in historical terms—and they accomplished the task in less than a hundred years' time.

Pierre Manent, the contemporary French political philosopher, has described the development and succession of political "forms" in Western history, from the city to the empire to the nation-state down to the formless though tightly governed post-modern era. "At a certain time," Manent writes,

> Europeans decided to do something new, something ab-
> solutely unprecedented, which appeared as the modern,
> which they called modern, and by which they distinguished
> themselves or separated themselves from everything previous.
> The very idea of the modern thus refers to a proposition, to
> a project that was embraced in hope by a larger and larger
> part of European opinion, to an enterprise that progressively
> rose in power before winning all of Europe and finally the
> whole world. This is what happened beginning at least in the
> seventeenth century. Something radically new was trying to
> come forth; then it came forth, defined itself, and imposed
> itself ever more imperiously.

This project was modernity, concentrating on political freedom and the rights of man. The United States was a relatively late result of this project, in which the Framers were sophisticated partners (which is *not* to concede that America is what neoconservatives describe as "dedicated to a princi- ple"). "After the [modern] revolution," Manent continues, "in the first half of the 19th century, there is a reflection on the best ways to put the princi- ples to work, and there is an analysis of the effects of the new order, some- times expected and unwanted." Manent argues that during the post-modern era, the era of the religion of humanity and of human rights, the modern form has been effectively abandoned as the nation ceased to represent the Western political ideal and was replaced by the idea of a bor- derless world of undifferentiated humanity and of sameness, a world cen- tered on "values" and "facts" that has replaced "active and concrete association" with the identification of the West with the "other"—no one to fight with, no one to love; a world in which "action consists in the strange suspension of action" in the belief that "our inaction will become more and more irresistible for ourselves and for those around us." As a Frenchman and a European, Manent underestimates how much of the initiative for the post-modern project came from America, rahter than the Continent.

Masonry, socialism, communism, anarchism, syndicalism, fascism, and nihilism are European inventions; Transcendentalism, Thoreau, Whitman, Christian Science, Dr. Norman Vincent Peale, Timothy Leary, and Transhumanism are American phenomena. (Nietzsche, who called on individuals to revolutionize themselves instead of their societies and live under a law of their own making, arguably belongs with these.) Historically, European reformers have aimed to "put their principles in common," as the Greeks said; to make reform a civic project. True to the spirit of American individualism, American enthusiasts have preferred to locate their intellectual and spiritual discoveries at the individual level, or that of the company of the happy few. (Each and every American, remember, is assumed to be "exceptional".) Self-help movements, self-renewal, self-invention and self-reinvention, self- transformation, self-transcendence originated for the most part in America, inspired by the characteristically American assurance of endless horizons, unrestricted capacities, complete malleability, and unlimited possibilities at the disposal of all citizens. Europeans have adopted these American attitudes to a limited extent, but one has the impression their hearts aren't really in it. In this respect, the difference between Europe and the United States is similar to the differences between the imaginative visions of two novels, Orwell's *1984* and Huxley's *Brave New World*, the first a European dystopia, the second an American one. The authors of both books were Englishmen, but while Huxley published his in 1937, five years before he moved to the American Southwest where he lived for most of the second half of his life, his insight into (and affinity for) the Californian brand of civilization allowed him the insight to imagine that the future nightmare would bear the American stamp, not the European one. (Critics generally agree that Huxley was a more accurate prophet than Orwell.)

The United States in the 21st century is Pierre Manent's modern project raised to a higher magnitude. Having set forth two and a half centuries ago with brash confidence to create an unparalleled country the likes of which the world had never seen nor scarcely imagined, she is now well along in the attempt to create a parallel universe with the eager cooperation of the Silicon Valley wizards who expect to replace reality with the virtual kind, diabolical doctors who manipulate human genes as if they were microchips and human tissue as if it were latex, and multiculturalist theorists who think that a man is a woman is a man is a hermaphrodite, the Ethiope is Rudyard Kipling, and East and West not only are not twain but never unmet in the first place. If this effort alone is sufficient to validate America's claim to exceptionalism, then indeed she *is* exceptional—for now at least, before the rest of the West, having accepted the challenge, catches up to her.

"Only what is not is beautiful," said Rousseau. Exceptional America agrees, and is doing her best to prove him right.

6. "Transparency" and Paralysis

"Democracy Dies in Darkness" is the motto of the *Washington Post*. The editors of the *Post* belong to the honorable group of which Norman Podhoretz once confessed himself a member: Idolaters of Democracy. And they are promoters of big government—that implacable enemy of democracy, or so democrats believed before the 1930s. No doubt the editors could demonstrate to their own satisfaction and that of their readers how the two things are really compatible. They would have a harder job explaining how democratic government is imperiled by the lack of the "transparency" liberals demand in every part of its machinery and every nook and cranny of its being. To conservatives, habitually skeptical of governments of scale, illimitable transparency should be a good thing, just as for perspicacious liberals it should seem a dangerous one. Yet conservatives, who fear anarchy as much as tyranny, should consider the possible paralysis of government functions a matter for equal concern.

"Nolite Confidere in Principibus"—"Do Not Put Your Trust in Princes"—is a healthy reminder of the truth of the saying that social and cultural problems do not have political solutions. On the other hand, princes and politics frequently cause social and cultural problems, exaggerate them, exploit them, and hinder and prevent the development of solutions for those same problems. Moreover, a dysfunctional political system is itself a social problem whose roots are frequently cultural and social. Yes, one ought not to trust in princes, but one can and should and must use them, curb them, and, occasionally, dethrone them. Political action presupposes imagining and choosing political means, and engaging in political activity. The need for counter-political activity

("reactionary" politics, as liberals understand it when the dominant institutions in society are liberal ones) implies an earlier defeat of the traditional cultures conservatives defend, as a hyper-politicized world is a triumph for modern post-liberal culture. Since the French Revolution, the left has been winning its war of 233 years against the right by elevating politics as the principal activity of modern Western societies—ahead even of commerce and professional sports—by the politicization of all human relationships, and of society itself. (The paradoxical converse—when everything is political, nothing is—is a rhetorical victory only, small comfort to anti-liberals or else simply irrelevant.) Obviously, the politicization of society demands a political strategy to reverse it; another paradox and an equally unfortunate one, the vast majority of people being temperamentally unsuited to politics and a politicized existence, as the history of societies ruled by ideological tyrannies shows. Advanced liberalism, which is entirely incompatible with the fixed human nature it denies, faces mounting resistance in the 21st century by roughly fifty percent of the Western populations subject to the rule of the international liberal regime. Under liberalism's sway, cultural resistance is officially discouraged or simply outlawed by liberal governments, so the Resistance is inevitably a political movement. Government of the right kind, the proper size, and the appropriate limits is as necessary to the reestablishment and maintenance of traditional societies as government of the wrong sort is to the perpetuation of liberal democracy. The idea that government is a necessary human institution is a truism, but one that bears repetition in the context of some contemporary conservatives' claims (Patrick Deneen, for instance, and Rod Dreher) that cultural renewal can only be accomplished by local institutions—the town councils and county commissions, the churches, and the family, or by withdrawn and separated communities—paying scant attention to the reform of national politics and the federal government.

No one denies that an open society and public government operating mostly in full public view and in response to the will of the voting citizenry are equally necessary to democracy; indeed, they *are* democracy. But government conducted openly in its broader operations is not the same thing as government conducted in the omnipresent glare of publicity and the media's piercing LED torch lights that penetrate everywhere by means of digital technology and whose discoveries are instantly disseminated, discussed, and debated by journalists in the hyper-partisan and hyper-emotional political atmosphere for which the extreme ideological divides in Western countries, the United States especially, are only partly responsible; the rest of it being attributable to unceasing reports of political and administrative minutia that partisans hope will ruin the electoral prospects of the political opposition. Politicians on the right and the left extol transparency and encourage more of it when it helps them and their side, and denounce it and demand that it be made opaque in the name of national security, or whatnot, when it compromises them. But democracy is endangered as much by the light that blinds as by the darkness that obscures. And it is an excess of brightness that threatens democracy in the digitalized 21st century, not the Stygian night.

As Macbeth murdered sleep, and the French Jacobins murdered politics in their day, the digital revolution has murdered public peace, public security, and—most importantly perhaps—public certainty about anything at all. While the *Washington Post* predicts the coming of a new Dark Age bereft of democracy, the *New York Times* still prides itself after a century and a half on reporting "All the News That's Fit to Print." But readers today, even of the once-trusted *Times*, cannot be sure what is fit for print and what isn't, and it is obvious that the paper's reporters aren't sure either except when they neglect to print whatever they fear may hurt their cause and hurry to print what they expect will promote it. Some item or another is excitedly inserted into the next edition and produces a transient flurry of national or international attention before it is eclipsed in the public mind by another, often contradictory, story. Transparency, or what is passed off as transparent, and the media glare endanger democratic society almost as much as they do democratic government. Popular "knowing" too much about too many things is far more subversive of democracy than knowing too little; the evil combination of transparency and digitalized communication is destroying the public understanding of what is really going on in the public realm as surely as it is destroying the public peace. The historian John Lukacs has explained how what used to be called "public opinion" (the considered opinion of the educated elite) has almost disappeared and been

replaced by "public sentiment"; the unconsidered, unstable, ever mutable, and highly excitable feeling of the general public. Transparency is
the creature of digital distraction and self-immersion in trivia shared
by its dispensers as well as by its consumers; public figures "in the know"
and private individuals who never shook their congressman's hand.
Democracy is—or is said to be, or supposed to be—government for, by,
and of the people, but a people obsessed by fluff and their own emotional responses to negligible or false bits of "information," dishonestly
or mistakenly disseminated (who can tell the difference?), cannot be expected to participate responsibly or intelligently in the business of popular self-government.

Limitless "transparency," like limitless popular involvement, in government is a functional impossibility, as antidemocratic political theorists
and philosophers and practicing politicians—professional diplomats
most acutely—have recognized for millennia. As an ideal held up by a
new generation of democratic office holders and public servants, transparency (reinforced as a virtue by the threat of ever more intrusive technology) has the dangerous effect of making citizens progressively
distrustful of their elected and appointed public men and women, whom
they suspect of failing to keep them informed of everything they have
come to believe they have the right to be told about the workings of government and the public service, and increasingly frustrated, resentful,
and unhappy with whatever they manage to learn about public life. On
the other side, transparency has encouraged honest politicians who fear
they cannot effectively perform their legitimate duties in the harsh light
of omnipresent scrutiny to become increasingly devious—or dishonest,
or more dishonest—at work; thus further undermining popular confidence in politicians, civil servants, and democratic politics and institutions themselves when their behavior is disclosed.

Beneath it all—extreme partisanship, scientific technique, and instant mass communication through personal devices as well as the mass
media, their 24-hour news cycle and their insatiable hunger for hot stories and dramatic revelations, most of them ultimately trivial but always
damaging to someone—is the existential discontent and suspicion liberalism has instilled in America and other Western countries concerning
their governments, their societies, and their own lives. Westerners have

learned—actually they've been taught—to view contentment either as the culpably reactionary or simply lazy disposition of chumps who are willing to pretend they are not being had by "the system," while knowing that they really are. Liberal society is the first in history to mobilize itself on behalf of an agenda for solving "problems" instead of patiently coping with the conditions that all human societies have always had to contend with or adapt themselves to. Liberals understand society as a project to be realized at some infinitely receding point in the future, not the natural result of historical growth which they have neither the patience to understand nor the wisdom to respect. It is entirely to liberals' advantage to advance their program by encouraging people to form desires that cannot possibly be realized in this world (and often oughtn't to be in the next) and ask government to fulfill them directly, or face the consequences at the polls—or in the streets, a pre-technological mode of protest that nevertheless became wildly popular in the U.S. after the election and inauguration of Donald Trump. The mass march too has to do with transparency but transparency in reverse, the thing observed passing through in the opposite direction, from the ruled toward the rulers rather than in the opposite direction. Even here, transparency avails government and society little, as the spectacle of a couple of million raucous and sloppy fat women enhancing the obscene spectacle of their outward physical persons with the scatological scandal of their dress communicates precisely nothing beyond the fact that two million raucous and sloppy fat women, etc., etc. are unhappy with the way the world is, with the regard it has for them, and probably also with themselves. If that is transparency, so is a distortive mirror at a carnival reflecting loads of bussed-in freaks enjoying an outing from their institution.

What the *Post* calls "democracy" dies under many conditions. One of these is the condition of ignorance concerning what democracy is, and what it isn't.

Pierre Manent, in an essay "The Tragedy of the Republic" (*First Things*, May 2017), reminds us that the republican government in its true form is not, as moderns like to think, democratic but aristocratic. (Montesquieu described 17th and 18th century England as "a republic disguised under the form of monarchy.") Manent views the republic as "the regime that allows and encourages the most action." Following the line of argument he developed in a book of a few years ago, *Democracy Without Nations,* he asserts, "Today we expect from a republic the opposite of a republic. We demand from it the least possible action, or what we call 'freedom.' For us, freedom is a world without command or obedience. It is a world in which public action can neither begin nor commend anything." This is so because democrats demand that their representatives and governments act as totally disinterested agents in their work of governance. No one who "serves" should take anything away from his service, they believe. But, Manent objects, "Service to the republic cannot be disinterested, because it is paid for by what is most precious in the eyes of ambitious citizens, that is, the honors granted by the republic, which boil down to public esteem. It is not disinterestedness that we should be asking of those who govern us, but rather ambition. It has been too long since we had the rare benefit of being governed by truly ambitious statesmen. The conviction has taken hold that our regime would be more republican if it ignored political rule still more. Political leaders are to serve our interests rather than commend our collective actions. The reigning social philosophy postulates the power and self-sufficiency of a spontaneous social form that would bring together order and freedom without the mediation of political rule. This is to abandon society to its inertia, that is, its corruption." So "When one opens the polls to decide who will have the honor of not acting, rivalries can be lively and passions virulent, but the men and women who fear ruling all look alike. Paralysis and stasis are taking hold and sinking roots, with the fervent help of citizens who demand action—and protest at the first sign of it."

In Manent's insight we find at once the meaning of, and the explanation for, the passion of the democratic left for "transparency" in government, an obsession compounded of the popular jealousy and resentment of people in high places who stand to take something from their service while finding personal enjoyment and fulfillment in the exercise of the powers legally and constitutionally granted to them by the electorate. And when the people elected to "power" are as violently disliked by the political opposition as they are today, the jealousy and the resentment become, literally, uncontrollable. Trump, in the short run at least, stood to lose, not gain, financially from his four year term as the nation's Chief Executive, a fact that made the Democratic representation of his connections and actions as "conflict of interest" a hypocritical sideshow. Yet even in the absence of the president's hostility toward Democratic "core values" and liberal "ideals," it is likely that whoever was elected to follow Barack Obama would have been challenged (as Obama himself was, though mildly) by the organized ideological advocates of "transparency," which might be defined, to paraphrase H.L. Mencken, as the sick feeling that someone, somewhere in government is exercising public power to accomplish something necessary and important, and receiving his just reward for doing so.

7. Self, Secularism, and Suicide

The response of the Western European governments, and of a substantial portion of what is called the European "elite"—roughly speaking, the upper-middle classes—to the invasion of the Continent from the East and South must be among the most unusual, and perverse, spectacles in human history. For nearly a year, the world looked on with astounding lack of surprise and seeming uninterest as the collective leaders of the greatest civilization in history abdicated their constitutional and moral responsibilities by refusing to defend their territories, their citizens, and their cultures against raw foreign aggression—even, in the case of Germany, inviting the aggressors to do their worst. What is happening in Europe today—currently the invasion of England by "migrants" coming in boats across the channel from France—seems unbelievable in the historic context, but it is happening, and very rapidly, too. By early spring of 2016 plain signs of popular resistance to the various national governments, the federal government in Brussels, and the "migrants" themselves were appearing across Europe—Eastern Europe especially—incited by the often disruptive, demanding, and arrogant arrivals, by the Muslim suicide bombings in Paris and Brussels, and by the fear of future bombings elsewhere on the Continent and in the British Isles. These reactions, though expectable and wholly natural, will be of far less interest to future historians than the policymakers whose actions they seek to reverse. The Continental elites' refusal to recognize the existential peril is impossible to explain as anything but a form of liberal psychosis afflicting the ruling class.

It is true that the Western world has been lacerating and mutilating itself from the time of Napoleon, and since 1945 it has been committing slow suicide. While acts of self-destruction of the first sort are the chronological story of every civilization from the beginning of recorded time, those of the second, so far as I know, are unprecedented in history. Why are they happening now, and why should the willing suicide be the most successful and powerful civilization the world has ever known? The explanation must take into account all the motives for suicide common to individual human beings: unbearable pain of one sort or another, the desire to punish others, self-loathing, despair. Yet while personal self-hatred and suicide are ordinary enough, self-loathing on a civilizational scale is without precedent and mass suicide almost so—and then in groups of mere hundreds, such as the People's Temple in Africa in 1978, rather than of scores of millions of successful and affluent people in dozens of nations. We are, it is true, speaking here of cultural, not physical, suicide, but the first is certain to end eventually in the second, facilitated by the enemies of the West who arrive in time to finish the job. At any rate the question remains: Why is what is happening in the West today, happening?

Western society is the only civilization ever to have renounced *voluntarily* its formative religious beliefs and abandoned *voluntarily* its sustaining religious traditions—unlike the Chinese whose official class first did away with historical Confucianism in the 20th century and less than a half-century later replaced it with Maoism, or the Russians, whose revolutionary government outlawed the Russian Orthodox Church and every other branch of Christianity and replaced it with Marxist-Leninism after 1917. In the nations of the West, by contrast, secularization, prolonged over centuries, was not enforced by government fiat, but instead promoted by the citizens themselves. Although the totalitarian governments imposed official public atheism on their countries, aggressive secularism could not extirpate private worship in secret as believing Christians (and Muslims, and others) took their faith underground. In the post-modern West, where post-Christian secularism is a popular phenomenon (despite its utility to post-democratic governments), no place remains for the Christian remnant save the churches themselves and these are increasingly beleaguered by secular government, supported in their punitive and exclusionary actions by secular activists. In the West, it is a case of religious all, or religious nothing: Church-going by committed Christians is still permitted, but beyond the churches there is no force that encourages committed secularists to experience the dimmest or most visceral flicker of Christianity, and everything to discourage and smother it. In the Soviet Union and the People's Republic of China, there was always a broad Christian Resistance stirring in the catacombs beneath the political and social surface of society. In the West today, no such thing exists. The religious faithful remain in public view but in shrinking numbers, harassed today and likely to be actively persecuted in the future.

Yet the situation is more complicated than militant secularists and the churches militant think, for reasons a good Darwinist should find easy to comprehend as the laws of mental and social evolution are at work here. As Chesterton said, no return to paganism is possible for the post-Christian world: having learned so much from its experience of two millennia of Christianity and gained so many graces from it, it cannot re-embrace the pagan cosmology in the state of innocence and ignorance in which it received it the first time. A corollary of Chesterton's argument is that Western atheists, agnostics, and religiously indifferent people generally have been influenced a great deal more by Christian belief, intellectual traditions, and social mores than they know, and certainly more than they would care to admit. They are creatures shaped by a moral, intellectual, and social evolution they can no more resist than fishes that have grown legs over countless generations can rid themselves of them in the coming ones. Christianity became a part of their evolutionary nature over two thousand years, without their agreeing to the process or even recognizing it. Their self-understanding, like their biological knowledge of their own species, has been formed in a complex Christian context they cannot reject without becoming confused, unsure, and intellectually and philosophically un-tethered; unable to recognize themselves, other people, or society for what they really are.

The post-Christian West owes Christianity its concepts of personhood, the value of the individual, stewardship, charity, self-sacrifice, self-transcendence, and the symbols that represent them in largely secularized feast days and other observances; and in poetry, painting, sculpture, architecture, and music, where they retain their subliminal power despite a waning awareness of their origins and the realities they point to. Darwinian scientism explains, if only analogically, how these symbols have become an integral part of the Western makeup; modern psychology their latent, involuntary, and often unconscious influence. Post-Christians may refuse all they like to believe and worship as Christians, but they cannot stop thinking and feeling in the cultural terms in which their ancestors thought and felt. Nor can they avoid feelings of emptiness, incompleteness, and even a vague sense of guilt in resisting these thoughts and feelings.

Having repudiated their identity as Christians, post-Christians in the West have been casting about for the past two centuries for some satisfying and supposedly valid form of self-identity other than the Christian identity. The most obvious and easily accessible of these forms is "liberal," liberalism being in part a secularized version of Christianity. Post-liberalism offers alternative identities, among them sexual, economic, educational, and occupational ones, but these are too narrow and individualistic to be ultimately satisfying. Pierre Manent argues that liberals' present attitude toward Islam and Muslims has nothing to do with Islam and Mohammedans as they actually are, but only reflects the liberal attitude itself. Liberals have no real interest in "the Other," either as a religious culture or as threat to the survival of the West, but only in maintaining the ideological purity of liberal ideals when confronted by that threat. The contrast between Europe's response to Muslim aggression in Germany and the Greek islands in the 21st century and its answer to the Sultan's navy at Lepanto in the 16th century, when the Europeans recognized the Moors' aggression as the religiously motivated geopolitical challenge that it was and met it accordingly, reveals the difference between modern ideology—the phony religion—and the thing itself.

Men find self-recognition and self-meaning only through self-identity of the most fundamental and significant sort: as *Homo sapiens* first and secondly as *Homo sapiens venerens* within the context of a particular and developed religion. Deprived of religion, men resort to subordinate forms of identity, ranging from the secondary (nationality) through the trivial (political affiliation) to the absurd (sexual "orientation," sexual "preference"). To be a religious person is to follow the teachings of a certain religion, to honor its theological ideals, and to try one's best to live up to them. Secular liberals honor what they call "ethical" ideals, and many do indeed attempt to realize them in their lives. The problem for liberals is that they are unable to codify these ideals in a morally and intellectually comprehensive system as complete and humanly satisfying as the Christian religion—divinely inspired rather than an invention of men—is satisfying. Liberals want a religion without religion, the "Church of Christ without Christ." They want a People of God with neither a god nor a people, and a people with neither a nation nor a broader civilization behind it; since modern liberals view religious, cultural, and national particularities as exclusive and hence illiberal.

Today the secular liberal West is undergoing the lingering experience of its lost Christian self—a phantom thing, like an amputee's leg, but in this instance the amputee is self-mutilated. He senses that some critical part of him is missing but, being self-blinded also, he cannot tell which part, and casts about for some artificial replacement to fill the space. He vaguely senses the phantom body hovering round, like the soul the ancient Jews believed remained in the presence of the corpse for four days after death, but his willed inability to apprehend spiritual reality leaves him profoundly unhappy, despairing, and filled with futile anger and self-loathing.

And this is understandable. Because where does the post-Christian man, and post-Christian West, go from here? After Christianity—the *ne plus ultra* of all religions, as Chesterton said—what religion? After Christian civilization, what civilization? After such knowledge forgiveness, what? asked Mr. Eliot. Finally, separated from the religious concept of the soul, what self? Manifestly despair, and the despairing self: the black, self-hating, self-destructive, and blasphemous despair that drove Judas to go and hang himself—the despair that comes only from guilt, recognized or simply sensed, that for a century now has been tempting what once was Christendom to mass spiritual suicide. Better ultimately for the soul of the West, perhaps, had Communism won the Cold War and imposed by force, for a chastening salubrious period, the official atheism it has since determined voluntarily to impose upon itself, before dying at last by its own hand.

8. Class and Identity

Modern liberalism is an organized, coordinated, and aggressive assault on human society and the human race. Its perverted, officially imposed, and relentlessly enforced understanding of humanity has sundered over the past half-century the historical connections between traditional societies and contemporary ones to the extent that the break between past civilizations and the modern pseudo-ones is very likely irreparable— an accomplishment the destroyers of the classical civilization of the West, whose medieval and early modern successors evolved organically from it as substantially the same civilization raised to a higher power, failed to achieve. If it seems unimaginable today that anything comparable to the former civilizations distinguished by their reverence for tradition, patrician values, standards and tastes, intellectual and artistic seriousness, sensitivity to the natural harmonies, their idea of leisure as the opportunity for gentlemanly pursuits rather than the playtime of proles rich and poor—all these things given meaning by faith and sustained by a coherent social order—can ever be realized again, it is because absolutely nothing in the world of the 21st century offers so much as a hint at such a future, while all signs indicate the opposite. The large mass of men today, for whom "civilization" has no meaning except in the liberal sense of the term, nevertheless are conscious, in their vague unconscious way, of a vast, unsettling, and unnerving void that can be filled only by the return of the old human realities that liberalism has banished from the world, foremost among them the natural human reality formerly signified by the word "class"—class, that is, in the healthy, pre-Marxian sense of the word.

For two or three centuries, liberals have promised to rid the world of a host of supposed evils, among them religious faith, guilt, suffering, sacrifice, inequality of wealth and position—and the class system. The world being what it is, so far as liberalism has succeeded in banishing these things most of them have managed to return by the back door and under cover of darkness. But, unlike Horace's nature driven out by the pitchfork, they made their return in grotesque, distorted, and unnatural forms, including materialist superstition, moral relativism, ideology, egalitarianism, socialism, neurosis, and, most recently, a new identitarian system to replace the old class one.

Historically, class distinctions have been the equivalent of original sin for liberals, and even the American Founders, who were neither liberals in the modern sense nor levelers, proscribed titles, whether hereditary or for life, from their new republic, though nearly all of them represented the upper levels of society. The French Revolution commenced the same year Washington was inaugurated as president, and what had begun as a convocation of the Estates General became in short order a comprehensive attempt to exterminate the French aristocracy in a program we should call genocide today. A half century later Continental Europe was engulfed by revolution from below, and Marx and Engels explained all of history as the dialectical process of the exploitation of the peasant and the proletarian classes by the owners of the means of production, and the final triumph by the former two over their oppressors. Since the middle of the 19th century, the history of the West, and more recently the rest of the world, has been mainly a process of social leveling-down to a more or less uniform social topography where what remains of the old aristocracy enjoys no more than celebrity status and the plutocracy, despite its lavish style of living, remains, socially and culturally, part of the mass society into which most of it was born. In cultural terms the modern liberal world is a classless though economically and educationally differentiated society, in which everybody looks and dresses and thinks and amuses himself like everyone else, no one is servant or master to another (though masters continue to hire servants, and servants to work for them), and all are democratic equals, while each citizen secretly considers himself king, as the French political philosopher Claude Polin argued.

Liberals consider the new classless society one of their major accomplishments, though an unfinished one. (Liberalism is the political agendum that can never be realized, as happiness is the human one.) Nevertheless, the abolition of class distinctions is running up against the ineradicable and insuperable need human beings have for distinctions of one sort or another, and for a sense of identity. These days the term "identitarian" signifies white nationalists in the United States and in Europe, yet it describes just as well people who identify themselves existentially as "woman," "black," "Hispanic," "mixed race," "gay," "transgender," "cis-gender," "Ivy League," "Ph.D.," "Democrat," "Republican," "liberal," "progressive," "radical," "conservative," or a member of some other proudly sensitive and defiant category of psychologically damaged or simply incomplete human beings. As "democratic" Americans in the 19th century filled the void left by class, rank, title, aristocratic clubs, and military orders with the Benevolent and Protective Order of Elks and the Eagles, the Sons and Daughters of the American Revolution, the Knights of Columbus, and similar grand-sounding organizations, so post-democratic Americans in an egalitarian society bereft of recognized social distinctions have invented new and even more frivolous and bizarre identities for themselves.

Liberals consider recent forms of self-conscious identity infinitely preferable to the old class consciousness, though they have not entirely abandoned the notion of class solidarity they borrowed from Marxism in the 1930s. So far as their ideal is social equality, cohesiveness, and the brotherhood of men, however, they see falsely. Whatever liberals think, the class system is an associative conceptual arrangement that promotes social integration and social order, while resisting a dissociative and atomizing one. Class is a fundamentally social principle, not an anti-social one, that bonds like people with like, while binding them in a functional relationship with subordinate and equally bonded likes arranged hierarchically in an organic social system. The class principle was made for human society, which explains why it has been so widely prevalent in history and why it persisted for so long, and still does in many modern instances. Liberals have claimed from the beginning that the class structure suppresses what they call "social consciousness," or "a social conscience," and even prevents it from forming. Yet the opposite is actually true. A very good recent book—*In Defense of Aristocracy*—by the English journalist, Sir Peregrine Worsthorne, suggests how this works. One way in which it does so, besides encouraging social cohesiveness, is by promoting intellectual excellence and coherence in the present day and in sustaining the continuity between past and present that has been destroyed by the discontinuities effected by liberalism.

Indentitarianism, on the other hand, is not a cohesive principle at all; it is a centrifugal agent of social and intellectual fragmentation, self-centeredness, narcissism, selfishness, and aggression that aggravates democracy's natural tendency to encourage each citizen to imagine himself the center of the democratic universe to whom his democratic "equals" ought rightly to bend the knee. Indentitarianism, whether racial, sexual, or otherwise, further encourages men and women to live starkly individuated existences characteristic of people who, because they define themselves by race, sexual preference, or some other insignificant or trivial characteristic, pursue single-issue lives rather than complete human ones—the exact opposite of Walt Whitman who contained within himself (as he thought) worlds. Single life cuts people off from each other, from their contemporaries, from the past and from history, and from the future. Whatever an agglomeration of such-minded people might be, it certainly isn't a society, since every true society—like the pudding Winston Churchill wasn't served—must have a theme, as every previous human society known to history has had one. But modern, liberal, individualist, relativistic, and classless societies necessarily lack theme, or character, because it is an upper class that provides society with both—to which the lower orders naturally contribute something of their own. The New Modern Society, lacking thematic principles and the social structure that generates and sustains them, is tautologically "unsustainable," as liberals say. (Ironically, "unsustainable" is among their god-terms—like "love," the ubiquitous reference to which underscores the prevailing absence of the thing it signifies.)

The modern democratic hostility to forms—men and women are changeable and interchangeable; a man can be a woman, and vice versa; dress that is appropriate to a beach party is equally acceptable at a funeral service—makes classification impossible. But without classification (one thinks of Aristotle) mental and social order are also impossible. Liberals would argue that identity is itself a form of classification, but if so it is a false one: In the liberal mind, a heterosexual can become a homosexual, who can then reinvent himself as a transgendered person, and return finally, should he choose to do so, to being a heterosexual male. This is not in the least comparable to a commoner being created a baronet and later elevated to the rank of earl, or the daughter of a couple that made a fortune in party favors marrying a prince of the realm with the near certainty that she will one day become its queen.

Liberalism has been fortunate in the sloppy laziness of the democratic masses (for which it is largely responsible) that has facilitated the carelessness regarding form by means of which liberalism has been able to impose itself upon popular culture, and what remains of the high culture. But it cannot suppress the innately human desire for the sort of distinctive, articulated social and personal identity that liberal society discourages in all its normal, healthy, and traditional forms; and as modern society ages further and grows increasingly economically stratified even as it becomes more socially monolithic, it may eventually be compelled to recognize the age-old human reality of class. Should it ever do so, that would be a very long step toward restoring an ordered, coherent, fully human society—not in itself the equivalent of the historical civilization liberalism wrecked, but perhaps the basis for something like it sometime in the far-off future.

9. *Kultur* and Culture

The historical controversy about who bears the blame for the outbreak of war in 1914 will never be settled. Too many of the participants contributed to igniting the catastrophe. German rearmament and the Kaiser's determination to build a navy equal to Great Britain's, the country's territorial ambitions on the Continent and abroad, and its militaristic spirit have been cited for a century as the war's principal causes. In a more general way, German *Kultur*—which German writers and politicians of the late 19th and early 20th centuries proudly distinguished from the rest of world *Zivilization*—was more important than any of these things, being fundamental to them. The essential importance of the myth of *Kultur* and of the "special path" its adherents and promoters believed it offered the German people is emphasized by Willi Jasper, a modern German scholar, in an excellent book, *Lusitania: The Cultural History of a Catastrophe,* which investigates the moral and cultural atmosphere conducive to the murder by U-boat of 1,197 civilians aboard a great British liner with an international passenger list.

While the great majority of Europeans in 1914 greeted the war with patriotic rejoicing, the Germans (Jaspers notes) outdid everyone else in the fervency of their jubilation. Earlier, Freud had diagnosed a death wish in the modern German soul that seemed to him to indicate the re-barbarization of Germany; later, Clemenceau observed that, "The German loves war as a form of self-love and because a bloodbath awaits him at the end. The German welcomes that end as if it were his dearest friend." In fact, a good deal more was involved in the business than abnormal psychology. The slow formation of middle-class democracy in Germany relative to what had already occurred in France and Great Britain gave the German intellectual elite far greater influence than educated elites elsewhere enjoyed, and this class was keen to invest the war with a philosophical and indeed a religious import, notably by endowing Goethe's *Faust* with military significance. (*The Military Faust* appeared anonymously in 1891, and a "Knapsack *Faust*" was distributed to the German troops during the war.) A restless and bored generation that had experienced nothing but peace since the Franco-Prussian War of 1870–71 was susceptible to such ideas, which seemed to reproach them for their indifference to the evils of the wider technological and materialist "civilization" they found meaningless and infinitely inferior to Germany's proud cultural tradition. Ernst Jünger, for example, complained that "We have branched out in too many directions." "It is on the tightrope walk between being and non-being that the true man reveals himself," he insisted, "for here his fragmentation becomes whole again, merging together in a few subversive activities of violent force. All the variety inherent in each and every form is reduced to a single meaning: battle." Several months after the war commenced, 93 artists, academics, and intellectuals undersigned a manifesto, "To the World of Culture," which claimed a proudly defensive role for Germany's role in the hostilities. "Nor is it true that the struggle to defeat our so-called militarism is not also a struggle to overthrow our culture, as our enemies hypocritically claim. Without German militarism, German culture would long since have been wiped from the face of the earth. German militarism has emerged from German culture in order to protect it in a country that for centuries has been plagued like no other by pillaging raids." To the majority of the German people, the war was a violent exercise in the Romantic and Kantian nationalist spirit of the previous century, pitting the "*Deutschtum*" against French democracy and British liberalism, culture against Western civilization. For them, the German army was fighting on behalf of "national greatness" and the God-given destiny of the Teutonic race to rule in Europe—and beyond.

To men and women of the 21st century, such claims are more than Romantic. They are medieval, even barbaric. The unpleasant truth is that they were mirrored, in altered form, in the justifications the Allied powers—the United States especially—offered for their participation in the Great War; the principle difference being that while Germany's propagandistic defense was nationally and culturally particularistic, that of the Allies—again, the United States especially—was international and abstract, the imperative to defend and promote World Democracy. Of course, everyone understood that "World Democracy" meant "American Democracy" extended across the Western nations, exactly as Germany wished *Deutschtum*, or its spirit, to be spread. Indeed, President Wilson's vision of the democratic ideal was in its abstract way as Teutonically absolutist as any the Germans imagined and tried to establish. Yet Germany's "ideas of 1914," like France's of 1789 and America's of 1917, have, besides the historical one, an immediately contemporary parallel: Washington's "ideas of 1991," and since.

The comparison, naturally, is not an exact one. Today's American political and cultural elite do not speak and act in the name of Anglo-Saxon democracy, or of American Anglo-Saxons, or even of Americans at all, as Woodrow Wilson did, and as the German elite acted and spoke in the name of the Teutonic race. They are far too inclusive, nonspecific, and abstract to identify themselves and their political ends in racial or cultural terms. Above all, they are far too canny to commit any such posy-modern heresy. They speak, instead, as globalists, humanitarians, democrats, cultural relativists, and equalizers, to America and to the world. But when addressing a domestic audience, they appeal to the great ideal that was also Imperial Germany's: the vision of national greatness shared by the Democrats, the Republican establishment, and the neo-conservatives—though not, in spite of his campaign slogan, by Donald Trump, whose strong isolationist tendencies reflect his rejection of political angelism and his commitment to "America First." Every other American president since George H.W. Bush has been *Kaiserlich* on American national greatness as the keystone in a future globalist construction.

Like the intellectual, political, and military elites in Imperial Germany before 1914, their American counterparts of the early 21st century are convinced of the superiority of their national culture, of the justness of the international mission national superiority confers upon it, and of its historical destiny to dominate and to lead the world. The Germans thought war was the means by which their destiny would be fulfilled. The present American establishment—the part of it located within the Deep State—thinks peaceful example preferable to war, but it is demonstrably willing to employ military force if example, moral exhortation, and cajolery fail to accomplish its international agenda. Like the imperial Germans, the imperial Americans appeal to their national histories and to the metaphysical idealism and popular national mythology they imagine shaped those histories. Both parties subordinate religious faith to secular idealism, though patriotic Americans and their government frequently appeal to pseudo-Christian ideas and the rhetoric of a denatured Christianity on behalf of the patriotic cause, as imperial Germans and the German government cultivated the support of the Catholic Church, the Evangelical Church, and even the synagogues. The obvious difference between them is that early in the 20th century "Christendom" still adhered to substantive Christian faith, while a century later America's official religion is Christian universalism without Christianity. And while the invocation of Christianity, whether of the Roman or the Lutheran kind, was immensely useful to Germany from the late 19th century down to 1918, today American belligerents' adversion to universalist ideals professedly uncontaminated by nationalist interests, material and otherwise, is more useful still. Imperial Germany pursued hegemony in the name of German nationalism; imperial America pursues the same goal under the auspices of internationalism. This is a more than a sly game played by our lords and masters—the would-be Masters of the Universe—in Washington, but the end is the same and so are the means, which are in the last resort military ones.

The intent is to disguise "Americanism" and "American values" as "universalism" and "universal values" when the latter are invoked by Washington's Americanized allies and by its kept pugs and satrapies in the Middle East and elsewhere. Had the imperial Germans proceeded before and after 1914 using the same strategy, they might have got a great deal further than they actually did. But that would have meant abandoning their claim to national and cultural superiority, something they were both too proud and too honest to do—unlike America's devious, dishonest, greedy, power-hungry, and hypocritical ruling class. The difference is between the behavior of proud and honorable Prussian Junkers and that of grasping ignoble Snopeses, of lecherous bullying Elmer Gantrys.

Pre-war Germans were, in many ways justly, proud of their *Kultur*. Officially speaking, twenty-first century America has no culture that is formally "ours." We are, supposedly, a culture created first in the melting pot and more recently by multiculturalism, a universal civilization founded on a set of abstract humanist and democratist "propositions." Ironically then, German 19th-century "*Kultur*" was a true historical "culture"—unlike the culture of 21st-century America, which is "*Kultur*" only in the pejorative aggressive sense in which anti-Germans for the past century have used the word. Woodrow Wilson took the United States to war in Europe to make the world safe for democracy. Since 1917, a long line of American presidents has done the same thing, not just on the Continent but around the world. The result of their interventions has been to make the world safe for what imperial Germans denigrated as soulless *Zivilisation*, dangerous to what they called culture—including the traditional American culture, which has been nearly annihilated in the bloody quest for the bloodless Universal.

Is 21st century America capable of an act of barbaric aggression comparable to the sinking of the *Lusitania?* Are our "leaders" capable of facing themselves in the mirror and recognizing Kaiser Wilhelm, Ludendorff, and Hindenburg, and the other German militarists Wilson and the rest of the Allied leaders condemned? There is ample raw material here for revisionist historians brave enough to accept the challenge to quarry.

CHAPTER THREE | THE POPULIST FALLACY

The Democrats and the rest of the left accepted the results of the election of 2016 with no better grace than they predicted the Republicans and the right would do if their man lost. The street riots, lawsuits, recounts and demands for more of them, constitutional challenges, furious denial, and refusal to accept the electoral decision in a spirit of peace and resignation—all these were what the Democratic politicians and the media warned the country to brace itself for in the event of Donald Trump's loss to Mrs. Clinton. They never really believed the opposite was possible (though John Durham, the Special Counsel for the U.S. Department of Justice by Attorney General William Barr, has since shown that her campaign was engaged in a criminal conspiracy to incriminate Trump for collusion with the Kremlin and throw the election). One understands why: for the left no battle is ever fairly or justly lost—or forgotten. After Obama's eight years in the Oval Office, it must have imagined that it had forged far enough ahead of the right in America's cold Civil War, and with sufficient momentum, that the opposition—the Enemy—could never overtake it and was thus condemned to outer darkness forever. The GOP's nomination of Trump as its candidate would have confirmed this expectation for them. Then, on November 8, the unthinkable happened. Understanding history as a dialectical process that advances by the laws of progressive rationality and enlightenment, the left does not appreciate the unexpected. And so the shock was a devastating one for them.

For liberals, Mrs. Clinton's motto, "Stronger Together," emblazoned on a blue background, became the equivalent of the Confederate Battle Flag of the Old South, the badge and symbol of their own lost cause. The left never accepts or even recognizes defeat; also, like the poor, it will always be with us. The day after Krugman's column calling the election "an outrage" that should be forgotten appeared, the *Times* published another Op-Ed piece suggesting that the winner-take-all laws under which the Electoral College acts are (after more than two and a quarter centuries) unconstitutional, arguing that members of the Electoral College in fact are free to vote their consciences, and noting "a new legal theory" that holds that "the courts" (the U.S. Supreme Court, presumably) could "give" the election to Hillary Clinton because the Russians had interfered in the elections. In the weeks after the voting, liberal critics at first, then the Democratic Party, went to work to discredit the President-elect at home and abroad by attempting to discredit the incoming administration. They knew they could not keep it from power, but they hoped to compromise it by establishing its victory in the popular imagination as illegitimate and "unfair" (the Russian hackers, Director Comey of the FBI, the Electoral College, the popular vote, and so on), presenting Trump's transition as chaotic, and the man himself temperamentally, even mentally and psychologically, unfit for the office of Chief Executive. The last time Democrats had made similar charges was during the electoral campaign of 1964, when they warned the country that President Barry Goldwater would incinerate daisy petals, small girls—the world. And the time before *that* was after President McKinley's assassination in 1901, when the elder statesmen of the GOP were horrified to discover "that damned cowboy in the White House." That the party of sweet reason, logic, and expertise is neither the party of rational debate nor of intellectual consistency is only one of many useful lessons from the election of 2016. Nor did it help that, as in the case of Brexit the previous June, the "wrong people" won. Indeed, for the left, that is probably the most "outrageous," as well as the most humiliating, aspect of the entire electoral catastrophe: an intolerable affront to the pride of the brightest and the best and to their "values" (in reality, mere working principles devised to facilitate the efficient management of liberal society, not a moral code rooted in transcendent belief) after months of being mocked, insulted, and defied by their inferiors along the campaign trail. "Merry Christmas, America!" following the election was, perhaps, the cruelest cut of all.

What liberals do not see, or refuse to see, or pretend not to see, is that Donald J. Trump is very far from being a reactionary person. He is, rather, a thoroughly modern one. He is also, however, a phenomenon of nature, which is only another way of saying that he is a faithful representative of natural man, Rousseau's man in nature—the "noble savage," as the French philosopher called him. The left, it seems, has grown shockingly conventional—bourgeois, in fact, in its old age. Modern liberals obviously imagine natural man as a liberal, meek and mild, not a reactionary wild man. But Trump is no more wild than he is reactionary, though he *is* unconventional—which, to liberals, who dislike and fear the unexpected, is almost as disruptive and objectionable. He has never intended to seize a post-modern country in a gorilla embrace and bear it, biting, scratching, and screaming, back into the Stone Age, or indeed any previous age; only to rectify certain of the excesses and mistakes of the contemporary world, in which he has thrived so spectacularly.

The democracy lived on, of course, to fight another day after Trump's election, but it had sustained grievous political and psychological wounds that its confident over-expectations in the final weeks of the election made especially painful. Yet the record of Barack Obama's two administrations, on which Mrs. Clinton chose to run, was not much to stand on or boast about. Bereft of positive substance and with far too much presidential sound and barely suppressed resentment, its roots were racial and cultural as well as ideological.

The departing president, in what felt to those who disagreed with him like eight interminable years in office, failed to fulfill every one of his campaign promises: to heal partisan divisions in Washington, reconcile the races, pull American troops from the Middle East and Western Asia, "reform" American immigration policy, create a functional system of national health care, abolish (or at least greatly reduce) the global stockpiles of nuclear weapons, strengthen America's relationship with its European allies (though they liked him personally better than they did George W. Bush), achieve the "pivot" to Asia, get the Trans-Pacific Partnership Act passed, and bring in a new Era of Hope and Change. Instead he gave up on Congress, the voters, and politics and resorted to getting what he wanted through executive orders, one of which he himself had previously called unconstitutional. Having accomplished so little of what he set out to do, Obama in retirement and his badly trounced party faced a future in which a significant amount of what he *had* accomplished was highly vulnerable to serious dismantlement by his successor, who promptly took advantage of the fact. To the left this was historical vandalism, an "outrageous" detour—perhaps a very long and damaging one—from the smoothly unfolding path of dialectically determined progressivism.

Only weeks before the presidential election of 2016 Mark Lilla, professor of humanities at Columbia University with a pedigree that includes previous affiliations with the University of Michigan, the John F. Kennedy School of Government at Harvard, New York University, the University of Chicago, *The Public Interest*, and the *New York Review of Books*, published *The Shipwrecked Mind: On Political Reaction*, a slight but unintentionally revealing work comprised chiefly of reworked essays that appeared first in *TNYRB*. One does not read very far in this slim volume before perceiving that by "reaction" and "reactionary" Professor Lilla means "religion" and "religiosity," to him greater threats to the American ship of state than all the icebergs, hurricanes, typhoons, tsunamis, treacherous capes, reefs, rocky promontories, and Scyllas and Charybdises combined.

Lilla takes a low view of, and is alarmed by, what he calls "cultural despair" and its supposed result, "apocalyptic history," and he deplores the "myths" and "Western mytho-histories" he thinks produce these things. "Why," he wonders, "do people feel the need for such myths? For the same reason people always have. We want the comfort, however cold, of thinking that we understand the present, while at the same time escaping full responsibility for the future." Myth, Lilla argues, promotes thinking in terms of more or less clearly defined historical epochs, in particular those "glorious" ones whose recovery *intacto* reactionaries believe necessary for the restoration of civilization. Lilla quotes Robert Musil, the Austrian writer and novelist: "A man cannot be angry at his own time without suffering some damage." But Christ was angry with much that distinguished His own time. So was St. Paul (who suffered "damage" in the form of "prison, scourgings, stonings, shipwreck, stonings, whippings and all manner of persecutions," as the prayer has it, in addition to the intellectual and psychological kinds Musil had in mind). So was every saint who followed him for two millennia. But Paul was not angry with *everything* in his time, and certainly he had no desire to return to a previous one, which in any case he did not regard as glorious. He looked forward instead to a future era in whose coming he had an unshakeable faith, however imperfectly he glimpsed it. Professor Lilla claims that "the radical nativist on the far right," like the radical Islamist, "despise[s] the present and dream[s] of stepping back in history to recover what [he] imagines was lost." Lilla doesn't consider why such people need to "step back in history" in order to recover some of it, when they can accomplish the same thing by moving forward while reaching behind themselves. No sane person denies that much of what is past is good, that much of what is good exists now only in the past, and ought to be retrieved and re-established in the present or that much in the present is bad, and needs to be removed. The left is all for removal (that, after all, is what liberalism has historically been about; until fairly recently it had been a program of reform, not of creating a newly imagined reality); why not some recovery as well? Does liberalism really hold that nothing from the past can be retrieved—even in renovated form ? Or that, if it can be, it should *not* be? Or that nothing in the past, which like the past is no longer with us, was any good at all?

For liberals of the present day, the answer to the last question seems to be, "Yes." Liberals believe that everything they have ever accomplished in the world has been unqualifiably for the better, and that not a single one of their achievements should ever be undone, repealed, or reversed. The left views any subsequent correction of liberalism's historical record as a shameful and unnecessary retreat along the forward march of history, and liberals are constitutionally incapable of voluntarily forfeiting the smallest measure of ground they have gained. The 62 million Americans who voted for Donald Trump in 2016, and the 74 million who did so four years later, believed that liberal government has exceeded all reasonable limits to create an over-powerful regulatory state, an unfair economy, and an intrusive and manipulative bureaucracy that together impose themselves upon, and insert themselves into, religious and educational institutions; interfere with traditional social patterns, norms, and arrangements established over millennia; set boundaries to freedom of speech and even thought; patronize and discourage religious faith and patriotism while aggressively promoting materialism, relativism, internationalism, and multiculturalism; and are working to realize an alternative world conducive to the interests of an elite constituted of the Establishment, the One (or Two, or Three) Percent. The designers and builders of this bloodless, insipid, but supposedly efficient new world inevitably view popular opposition as "reactionary," partly because these prophets of post-modernity—the "experts"—forgot long ago what reality looks like. But "reaction" is a false characterization of the force that is resisting them, which is simple common sense supported by the shared instinct of humanity.

If Donald Trump really *is* a reactionary, he must have an era in mind to "step back" into. But what era would that be? The 1980s? The 1950s? The 1920s? The pre-civil war period when America tolerated slavery and fought victorious battles against Indians and Mexican thieves and rapists? In fact Trump longs for no particular golden era, because, as a businessman, he doesn't think that way. He simply wants to live in an America that is recognizable from the history books and from his youth and that also hangs together somehow, an America that "works" again. He sees much that is wrong in contemporary America that he wishes to correct. A sufficient number of Americans agree with him to have got him elected president once. That was an "outrage" in the opinion of liberals who wish to take the country forward into to an experiment, at once hopelessly idealistic and viciously materialistic and power hungry, of the sort that has been attempted in past eras, every time with catastrophic results.

1. The Wellesley Zarathustra

"Laws [concerning 'reproductive health'] have to be backed up with resources and political will and deep-seated cultural codes, religious beliefs, and structural biases have to be changed." Thus spake Zarathustra at the Women in the World Summit in New York City in April 2017 at its annual celebration of the Transvaluation of All Values.

"Religious beliefs...have to be changed." In translation: "People whose religious beliefs disagree with the thinking of people inside this hall *must substitute opposing beliefs for the ones they have now.*" On penalty of what, Mrs. Clinton? The English Test Acts between 1661 and 1678 applied only to public officials who refused to take Communion from the Church of England, not to English private citizens. The lady herself probably had (and has today) no clear idea, although one may speculate on how she'd *like* to see recusant dissenters in post-Christian America who refuse to countenance, much less be implicated in, abortion, gay "marriage," and "transgender" operations for sexually confused persons as young as five or six, and are otherwise guilty of harboring dangerous "structural biases," dealt with in future. No doubt it isn't pretty, though probably less drastic than the remedial proceedings accorded "heretics" in the Tower during the reign of Elizabeth I, or at Guantanamo during the administrations of G.W. Bush and Barack Obama. Less pretty still than imagined horrors is the threat itself—a quiet warning of future menace unprecedented in American history. The Clintons liked to imagine they "made history" in the casual and effortless way ordinary couples make sausage and build pigpens, without ever having much to show for the claim—until April 2015, when the distaff partner went ahead and did it.

The Constitution of the United States prohibits "[any] law respecting an establishment of religion, or [denying] the free exercise thereof...." As is well known, a sentence in a private letter of Thomas Jefferson's adverting to "a wall of separation between church and state" led somehow to the clause's being misinterpreted to mean that church and state must be kept "separate," and in time to the belief that government at every level—federal, state, and local—is constitutionally obligated to oppose any religious influence upon society at all. Orestes Brownson explained the results of what he called the "political atheism" of the Founders (most of whom were not irreligious men, though deists) on the future status of religion in the United States, among them the popular assumption that religious belief is of no great importance to American society. But religion can be socially unimportant only when it has no interest or relevance for a society's individual citizens. Religious people naturally view—they cannot help viewing—the world and all that goes on in it, including government and other public business, through the lens of belief. John Henry Newman spoke against "an avowed doctrine maintained in this day, that religion has nothing at all to do with political matters; which will not be true till it is true that God does not govern the world, for as God rules in human affairs, so must His servants obey in them." To Newman's mind, "that multitude of matters which comes before us of a social nature... bids us have an *active* opinion about" them. Newman perceived a danger in a rapidly secularizing country that citizens who believed all public affairs should be conducted on religious principles might be discouraged by aggressive secularists from giving religiously informed opinions on such matters, and bullied into keeping those opinions to themselves.

Politics is essentially a moral activity, a proposition denied by few agnostics or even atheists who object, rather, that since moral principles are really religious ones for the pious, religiously minded people should not be allowed to express them in public debate in a secular society. The exception would be contributions by the religious left to the national debates, which are reliably 99 percent political leftism and one percent religious heresy.

Militant secularists and other enemies of religion for whatever reason are plainly justified in recognizing the involvement of religious men and women in political life, starting with the vote, as an intrusion of religious conviction into politics. The Catholic Church, for example, teaches that baptized Catholics are members of a transcendent institution, the Body of Christ; undeniably therefore, each and every Catholic, acting individually, is acting not just on behalf of but, in miniscule part, *as* the Church as well. But no secular defense against such intrusion is possible except to bar professing Catholics from any involvement in public life, as was English policy from the Reformation down to the Catholic Relief Act of 1829. So far, American secular liberals, partly from conscience, partly from philosophical consistency, partly from prudence, and very likely also from fear of bad publicity have refrained from taking the final step. But who knows how far liberals will go in the coming years—whether Hillary Clinton was pointing the way in her New York address, or not?

The relationhip between Christianity and the secular power has varied widely across two millennia. The early Church kept Her head down and tried to stay out of harm's way. After Constantine, the Augustine ideal was a kind of spiritual apartheid separating the City of God from the City of Man. During the early Middle Ages, the Church accepted the secular responsibilities of collapsed and disintegrated worldly powers and joined the City of Man with the City of God, a Kingdom of Two Thrones lasting several centuries in which secular and ecclesiastical powers were nearly indistinguishable. During the Reformation, Christianity was fractured by schism and divided into contending theological and ecclesiastical parties whose disagreements became secularized with the rise of the new confessional states so that religion and politics were fused once more, as they had been in the medieval period. Finally, during and after the French Revolution the Christian churches were assaulted by violent political atheism and persecution. Thus three different forces pressed Christianity into political action before the early 19th century: practical necessity, schism, and atheist aggression. Since then Christians have been confronted with a new and unprecedented threat: cooptation by liberal democratic society.

It is an historical cliché that democracy since 1789 amounts to Christian moral and social teaching desacralized, immanentized, and translated from personal terms into social and political ones, what Chesterton had in mind when he spoke of "Christian values gone mad." Modern democracy supplants the Christian model of godly government with the ideal of popular government under the special protection of an approving and indulgent democratic god, the Christian affirmation of the spiritual equality of all men before God by temporal equality imposed by universal suffrage, notions of the political and social equivalence of men, women, and cultures, and the idol of "human rights" (formerly the "Rights of Man"); Christ's insistence on a special regard for the poor, alms giving, and rendering unto Caesar what is Caesar's by the welfare state, the progressive income tax, and economic leveling; and "Suffer the little children to come unto me" by "the rights of the Child." Meanwhile, while Christian compassion is reinterpreted to justify—actually, to sanctify—practices condemned by Christian teaching, such as abortion, divorce, sodomy, and now homosexual marriage, as abominations. So long as democratic government was limited to the functions of government historically—providing for the national defense, husbanding the national wealth, preserving the rule of law—democratic philosophical, moral, and sentimental excess was not a direct problem for Christians. Scripture nowhere endorses written constitutions, the separation of powers, bicameral legislatures, free elections, trial by jury, *Habeas corpus*, freedom of contract, or taxation with representation, none of which is a question of faith and morals for any denomination. The Christian churches found themselves progressively at odds with government only as it expanded its powers and extended its reach in transforming itself into what Tocqueville called "an immense tutelary power...absolute, minute, regular, provident, and mild," vested with the responsibility "to secure [the citizens'] gratifications and watch over their fate." Over the past century and a half, democratic government has taken Christian social teaching out of the churches and codified it in secular law. The result is a reversion in secular terms to the practice of the Western ecclesiastical and confessional states, whose legal codes reflected and embodied canon and religious law—but there is one obvious difference.

Advanced liberal government has not adapted Christian law and morality to their own ends. It has hijacked them and substituted in their place the grotesque misapprehension and misrepresentation of the originals that advanced liberalism is trying to impose and impress on Western societies. Orthodox Christianity, where it has not been corrupted by the new post-Christian public religion, is in the difficult, uncomfortable, and increasingly dangerous position of being compelled by faith and conscience to correct its official caricature and stand up to the secular powers responsible for it.

Like all liberals, Mrs. Clinton believes (or pretends to believe) that Christians are attempting to "impose" their beliefs on nonbelievers, when the truth is precisely the opposite. Unbelievers generally and anti-Christians in particular, starting with secular government, are trying to impose *their* unbelief on Christians. The "wall of separation" is certainly under assault, but the people wielding the crowbars are on the anti-church side of that wall. Those who want to ban religion from public life, who wish to keep the churches, church people, and their beliefs and principles out of state and public business, and now out of private business and family and private life as well, must be made to understand that aggressive secular government, by intruding recklessly and relentlessly into spheres of life that were formerly influenced and often dominated by religion, guarantees that these spheres will become more and more matters of religious concern. The controversy regarding the proper relationship between state and church, believers and unbelievers, will only continue to expand and deepen, while growing increasingly more passionate. The advanced liberal state, by deliberately politicizing religious ground (as the left since Marcuse and the Frankfurt School has argued it should), has reciprocally imported religious zeal into the political life of post-modern nations. If the left wishes the churches to stay out of politics, it need only keep politics out of the churches by leaving them in peace to perform their sacral mission.

It is possible that Mrs. Clinton and her cohorts understand this. If so, their appearance of overlooking reality can mean only one thing. Liberals are eager to bring the existing tensions between political and religious interests to outright war because they are determined, and fully expect, to win it by any and all means necessary for the purpose.

2. The Populist Fallacy

The mood in Washington during the weeks leading up to the inauguration of Donald J. Trump combined the bloodthirsty rage of the Reign of Terror and the wild comedy of "A Night at the Opera" as the New Jesus and his holy family prepared to ascend by helicopter from the Capitol Building on January the twentieth following the swearing-in of the Anti-Christ. The judgment expressed by Andrés Manuel López Obrador following his defeat in the Mexican presidential election of 2006 perfectly conveys the mood of the Democrats, and of liberals generally: "The victory of the right is morally impossible."

Damaging as the political loss sustained across the board by the Democratic Party was, the symbolic affront by the Republican candidate to liberal "values," to liberal idols and orthodoxies, and to liberals themselves was in some ways more damaging still. Rep. John Lewis, a veteran of the civil rights demonstrations who was beaten and jailed in 1965 and now a liberal icon, expressed their sense of outraged *lèse majesté* when he stated publicly that the Donald Trump would be an "illegitimate" president. Though Lewis could not have delivered a greater symbolic insult to a President-elect than this one, Trump was instantly assaulted by swarms of enraged army ants for countering that Mr. Lewis would do better to look to the very real problems in his own district than challenge the results of the election on false grounds. "I don't think we have ever had a president so publicly condescending to what black politics means," a black professor of African Studies at Duke University told a reporter for the *New York Times*. "He doesn't feel the need to perform some sort of belief that [the civil rights movement] is important." The Lord rebuked St. Peter when he made an ass of himself, but a man of color whose claim to secular sainthood was established in Selma, Alabama, ranks several steps higher than the Fisher of Souls, and consequently stands for all time above reproach—never mind that it was a short step from Lewis's charge of Trump's illegitimacy to calling the choice of the 63 million voters who supported him "illegitimate" as well.

Tens of millions of the former President's admirers are well or highly educated, economically secure, and socially established people; over a third of them have at least college degrees. Nevertheless Trump has always been widely condemned as a "populist," a term not understood by the upper ranks of society as a compliment, though the historian Christopher Lasch thought populism the true voice of democracy. In *What Is Populism?*, Jan-Werner Müller describes it as "a degraded form of democracy that promises to make good on democracy's highest ideals ('Let the people rule!').... For populists," he continues, "there cannot be such a thing as legitimate competition when populists run for office.... [And w]hen they are in power, there can be no such thing as a legitimate opposition," since "populism is a particular *moralistic imagination of politics*." Müller's characterization ignores the historical fact that both the refusal to recognize the legitimacy of one's opposition *and* a moralistic form of political engagement have been displayed far more directly and unambiguously in the recent past by Americans who call themselves liberals than by those whom liberals call populists (or even conservatives), and that their views are the converse of Señor (now President) Obrador's belief that every conservative political victory is an immoral one. When Müller adds that populism is "a moralized form of anti-pluralism," he fancies himself on unequivocal grounds.

So what actually *is* populism? Müller properly distinguishes between populism of the American and European sorts. "In the United States, it is common to hear people speak of 'liberal populism,' whereas that expression in Europe would be a blatant contradiction, given the different understanding of both liberalism and populism on both sides of the Atlantic." He lists among the necessary elements of populism anti-elitism, identity politics in some form, anti-pluralism, opposition to diversity and what dissidents from liberalism see as "enemies of the people," and the intent to "hijack the state apparatus," including at the ballot box. Populism "tends to pose a danger to democracy," in part because populists "actually rely on a symbolic representation of the people"—though the description clearly applies with equal force to liberals, as the post-election protests across the country, and the world, show.

Populism has meant different things in different times and in different situations, though it is, indeed, *always* anti-establishment. So the nature of an establishment necessarily determines the nature of its populist opposition. Were the French, Russian, Mexican, and American Revolutions "populist?" (Müller considers the first possibility but only in an unsatisfactory way, as he denies that Rousseau's ideal society as an expression of the "general will" was "populist" without noting that Rousseau's model was Geneva, a small and homogeneous republic.) He quotes the Dutch political scientist Cas Mudde's definition of populism as an "illiberal response to undemocratic liberalism"—a negative *or* a positive description, depending on your opinion of modern liberalism. Most importantly, though, populism in its present usage is a term invented by one elite or another to discredit any opposition to the program devised and imposed by that elite. In the first two decades of the 21st century, populism in the Western world has simply meant revolt by disillusioned or old-fashioned liberals and democrats (as well as conservatives) against illiberal democracies and undemocratic liberals. Because populism, like any other political tendency or movement, is situational, it is usually only as good as the opposition is bad. But the Western left, which defines the term to suit its purposes, applies it to any political movement with broad (not necessarily majoritarian) popular support that either resists it, or that the left doesn't like. One of the principal uses of this rhetorical strategy is to avoid or deflect the question: Can "populist" mean simply "popular"? Can it be something other than an "ism"? The answer is it not only can be, it *is*—in Europe as well as in America.

What social and political conditions encourage populism and help shape its agenda? Müller answers, those created by the cultural and ethnic pluralism that liberal governments encourage. That being the case, can populist reaction against pluralism as a liberal political and social program ever be justified, politically and morally? Müller acknowledges popular resentment and anger arising from public frustration as an empirical fact, but hastens to qualify the concession when he adds, "that is not to say that all these reasons are plausible and should be accepted at face value," while nowhere mentioning that pluralism has been aggressively pursued for decades by Western liberals. The pluralist democracy opposed by contemporary populists is not the liberal form of liberal democracy of the pre-post-modernist past; it is the hyper-pluralist one promoted today by liberal governments throughout the West. Pluralism in the age of transformative multicultural mass immigration means something very different from what "pluralism" used to mean, and popular acceptance (often grudging in any case) of the older pluralism does not imply the same social and political consequences that acquiescence to the modern version does. Advanced liberalism systematically destroys a liberal social order that was already barely workable, and replaces it with a caricature that is not workable at all. And it is the caricature that populists today are resisting. Modern populism sets itself against advanced liberalism—liberalism gone mad. And this is the case too with Trumpism, which refuses to accept the new liberalism's reinvention of national (and human) reality. Trumpism is a natural human response to the smug arrogance of the liberal, or neoliberal, establishment, succinctly expressed by this passage from a recent article in the *New York Times* describing the World Economic Forum in Davos the week before Donald Trump's inauguration: "The growing electoral strength of populist, anti-European Union parties in France, the Netherlands, Italy, and Germany have [sic] intensified fears that the union may not endure. These developments have yielded a growing sense that a complex world is suddenly short of adult supervision." The correspondent for the *Times* recognized President Xi's address to the conference as a hint that China's policies of economic globalism would help to ensure that the world will be managed (in the reporter's gloss) by "serious-minded people…taking considered action to address consequential challenges…." This is the *porta-voce* of undemocratic liberalism speaking, the ruling liberal class that considers itself the sole "adult" and "serious-minded" presence in the world today: the new global establishment, in its earlier liberal incarnation, taught the peoples of the West to resist and rebel against those "undemocratic" establishments it called "conservative." This is a lesson it is no doubt regretting having taught them.

When one half of the United States is so far alienated from the other half that marriage between Democrats and Republicans is increasingly rare, "populist" rebellion is a wholly inadequate, and dishonest, explanation for the state of American politics today. Seeking to analyze Trump's inaugural address, the media found the key in "populism," a political phenomenon whose origins they erroneously traced from what Arthur Schlesinger, Jr. called "the Age of Jackson." In fact, the period was known to contemporaries as the reign of "The Democracy," the Democratic

Ascendancy. The word "populist" came into use in the United States only toward the end of the 19th century, with the founding of the Greenback Party in 1874 and, following it, the Populist Party in 1890.

On the morning that President Obama became former President Obama, he posted this message to the American public on Facebook: "the single most powerful word in our democracy is the word 'We.' 'We the People. We shall overcome.'" Obama does not think of himself a populist, nor is he one. (Surely, this wielder of the pen and the phone, the Master of the Executive Order, is no democrat, either.) Nor is President Trump, whose inaugural address several hours later was a Declaration of American Independence from the world and its unceasing demands on America, and a rededication of the nation to the security and welfare of the American people. That his address, like his words along the campaign trail, should be viewed by liberals as "populist"—racist, reactionary, ignorat, xenophobic, and an apathetic to government—only shows that they no longer understand what democracy properly is and should be. Trump and his "movement" are not populists. They are old-fashioned democrats of the kind that liberalism had driven almost to extinction—or thought it had. "Today," Jan-Werner Müller believes, "what will always need to be present [in populism] is *some* distinction between the morally pure people and their opponents." But it is modern liberals who assert their moral purity, not "populists;" the party of Hillary Clinton and Joe Biden, not of Donald Trump.

For Americans, Republicans and Democrats alike, the "Other" has become one-half of the country. America is in a state of cold civil war, to which notions of "populism"—and Trumpism as populism—are either irrelevant or, like the "populist-nationalist" advocacy initiative founded shortly before the inauguration by a group of former employees of *Breitbart*, unrepresentative of a broader movement. In the 1930s, the novelist John Dos Passos, then in his liberal phase (20 years later he became a contributor to *National Review)*, concluded in disgust and despair, "All right: We are two nations." Today America is still two nations, but in a different and far more dangerous sense. Then, the division Dos Passos perceived was social and economic. Three quarters of a century later the United States is really two worlds, two metaphysical realities inhabited by what seem almost to be two separate species.

3. Chesterfield and Chesterton

Much in life may come down to a choice between the respective views of Lord Chesterfield, who urged his son always to excel at whatever he did, and G.K. Chesterton, who once wrote that, "If a thing is worth doing, it's worth doing badly."

The issue, of course, is what the "thing" in question is. If it is a mere amusement, like social dancing or keraoki or hobby painting or Sunday afternoon poetizing or weekend shooting, Chesterton was right. If, on the other hand, it's professional ballet, or operatic singing, or painting on commission or writing for pay, or military marksmanship, Chesterfield was. A further issue is whether that thing is worth doing on a "serious," or professional, basis: ball playing, for example, or bowling, or swimming, or tennis, or golf, or any other sport, the essence of which is, or should be, the sheer joy of the thing itself rather than whatever tangible benefit may come from it. Chesterton also wrote: "I entertain a private suspicion that physical sports were much more really effective and beneficent when they were not taken quite so seriously. One of the first essentials of sport being healthy is that it should be delightful; it is rapidly becoming a false religion with austerities and prostrations." He failed to add that it was also in the process of becoming a major industry, whose tangible results include vast sums of money paid out to a great many people, beyond the athletes themselves.

The worth of doing something badly or not is ultimately a matter of discernment, determined by one's ability to distinguish between what truly is important in human terms and what isn't; it is a question of final values. Approached from this perspective, pushpin or football is the equal of singing *bel canto* at the level demanded by La Scala, or writing "The Four Quartets," or weaving a traditional Navajo rug. The problem here is that for modern pluralist-democratically minded people there are no ascertainable values, only imagined or, at best, relative ones. The way around or through this cultural impediment is to evaluate in an objective, rather than a subjective, manner the several elements of which a particular activity is composed. Professional football demands, beyond natural ability, physical strength and stamina induced by training, physical skills including speed, maneuverability and dexterity, superb hand-to-eye coordination, and a profound knowledge of the rules of the game.

Professional singing requires a voice of superior beauty and agility, an exquisite ear, physical stamina, endless vocal practice, sound training in music theory, basic competence as an actor and a sense of stage presence, the ability to sight-read, sing in parts, and to learn complex scores, in which a basic proficiency in piano is of great help. Beyond all of that lies the crucial intellectual component: the intellect, as distinct from intelligence, which cannot be taught but only cultivated. Intellect allows the singer to grasp the intent of the librettist and composer as well as how text and score complement each another, to interpret a work of art with a completeness and impact that can be achieved only by a superior musician endowed with, in addition to the other gifts, a profound human sensibility that, being largely instinctive, also cannot be taught but must be developed by years of experience and artistic development. As for poetry, it too depends upon, besides natural talent and a good ear, training (more likely self-training) in poetic structure (rhythm, scansion, rhyme, form, and so forth), and the movement of the intellect: wide learning in many fields, the gift of observation and the ability to represent what one sees, a powerful poetic imagination, human insight and understanding, and finally the ability to bring these things together in a unique work of art. When compared with singing and poetry, rug weaving, though indisputably requiring talent, skill, a sense of color, and inordinate patience is plainly a craft, distinguishable from the arts by the fact that the intellect is unnecessary to it, though certainly it may nevertheless be possessed by the craftsman.

The point of this disquisition is a simple one: The greater the part the intellect plays in any human activity, the less value there is in doing it badly (and the less excuse for that).

Since Chesterton's time, the view of Chesterfield has come to prevail, with bad effects that Chesterton himself apprehended. It ought to be obvious that to approach every activity every day as a quest for the Olympic gold or the Nobel Prize or an Oscar or the Prix Goncourt is unhealthy—but to contemporary people, it isn't. Consider, for example, exercise and physical fitness today, when it seems that the large majority of people who are not professional athletes either refuse to get up from a chair or make a fetish of "working out," rising hours before work to visit the gym, running marathons on the weekends, and taking lessons from certified trainers in how to develop this or that muscle group, one or another physical skill, by acquiring the right "technique." A generation or two ago, it would have occurred to few even of the most active people that physical exercise is something to be taught, that fitness is properly an academic subject to be studied, and with great solemnity. Exercise was simply *doing* something physical, and if it were done badly—*Quel différence?* One enjoyed the bodily activity, and felt the better for it, and *was* the better for it. Similarly with the out-of-doors. Thoreau, Theodore Roosevelt, Ernest Hemingway, and Edward Abbey went into the forests, the mountains, the plains to explore, observe, appreciate, enjoy, and even meditate upon the natural world, whose peace and solitude, as well as the opportunity for adventure and sometimes danger, was the point of it all. Today such people have been replaced almost entirely by competitive joggers, mountain bikers, dirt bikers, rock climbers, parachutists, kayakers, endurance riders, and marathon runners who seem to have little interest in the natural setting in which they pursue their sport but only in its special technique and their own performance—in *themselves*. Read any of Abbey's books, while trying to imagine him doing any of these things in Utah's Grand Gulch Canyon, The Maze, on the slopes of Tikhunikivats in the La Sal Mountains above Moab. Or Thoreau, in the woods and mountains of Massachusetts and New Hampshire and on the Maine rivers. Or Hemingway up in Michigan. These men enjoyed direct physical contact with the natural world, careless for the most part of whether they were "expert" in their engagement with it or not. (Though Hemingway was foolishly competitive in the field, the Rough Rider assessed himself as no better than an average shot.) Yet they were knowledgeable and proficient outdoorsmen, far better equipped to survive the onslaughts of nature than most mountain bikers knocked off their machines or runners caught by an unexpected snowstorm in the backcountry. Most importantly, Thoreau's *Walden*, John Muir's *My First Summer in the Sierra*, Abbey's *Desert Solitaire*, and Roosevelt's *Ranch Life and the Hunting Trail* were not the results of timed jogs and competitive group runs or horseback races along wilderness trails, but the artistic issue of long contemplative walks and other more vigorous explorations on foot, in the saddle, or by canoe in the beloved country, whatever and wherever it was.

Post-moderns have a horror of anything done "badly"—meaning for them "not as well as it might be done"—that helps explain their inordinate respect for and reliance upon "experts" in every field of human activity, from selecting a bottle of wine to rearing children to holding political office—and running for it. Since around the middle of the 19th century, when the push for a professional civil service was established in Great Britain and America, expertise earned through academic training and long practical experience, supported by an ethos of professionalism and careerism, have been thought necessary to a competent performance in public affairs, both political and administrative. The idea behind civil service "reform" was to flush out the "amateurs"—meaning, in Britain, second and third sons and their aristocratic relatives—from public life and replace them with "experts," including "scientific" experts. This prejudice in favor of the "expert" has only widened and solidified since then, no matter that the bureaucrats and public specialists the new regime embodied have been no more successful at governing than their blue-blooded predecessors: Arguably, they have been a good deal less so, when one considers the decline of Great Britain since 1914 and the gummy gelatinous maze the American public sphere has subsided into over the same period. Before the summer of 2016, professional politicians were credited with knowing at least how to manage such things as putting on national referenda and winning their personal electoral campaigns—until a wealthy British insurance tycoon and his friends succeeded in wrecking the plans of a Prime Minister by pulling off Brexit, an event followed five months later by the election to the presidency of an American tycoon with no political experience after he delivered a sound shellacking to the Chief Priestess of Wonkery, whose coronation had been expected by experts in the media and in the academy, all while spending a third of the money his opponent burned in the effort. These same experts agreed that the same tycoon campaigned in person as badly as the neophytes he hired for his staff ran the wider operation. But he won—having reveled in the battle, "unprofessionally" as it may have been prosecuted; and afterward, as President of the United States, he went a long way toward fulfilling the promises he made to his supporters during his campaign. One wonders what Chesterfield would have made of this. On the other hand, it is more than possible that GKC, the champion of the little man, would have enjoyed the spectacle immensely, despite his lack of sympathy for plutocrats.

The movement across the western democracies so inaccurately, and misleadingly, called "populism" is, among other things, a rejection of the expertise, scientism, and professionalism of the political and bureaucratic elites who insist that they, and they alone, are capable of doing all that needs to be done to maintain the power, the affluence, the security, even the continued existence of complex technocratic post-modern societies. "Populism," however, guarantees that elitist candidates for public office, and indeed any sort of government job, will be challenged by people who prefer to see the right things done more or less badly than the "wrong" ones done well. The history of political and public life has always been largely a matter of muddling through with the aid of circumstance, contingency, and simple luck, a business in which non-specialists and even amateurs have as good a shot at success as the "experts," technocrats, and planners whose best-laid plans have far more often than not been thwarted by the simplest events and run aground on the most ordinary human facts and existing social conditions. If the human race depended on sheer intellect and expertise, it would have gone extinct millennia ago.

During the Vietnamese War, liberals did not bother to disguise their faith in what one of their stellar lights memorably called "the best and the brightest." The phrase has hardly been heard since 1974, but the faith itself has not gone away. Instead it has been replaced by "the experts" who, though even less successful in war and peace than their famous predecessors, nonetheless pride themselves on their determination to excel at everything they put their hand to and to win every time, despite having so often lost in ways embarrassing to themselves and with dire consequences for their country. It is no mystery why populism should have arisen when it did and why populists themselves come from where they do.

4. The Loss of the Familiar

From the late 19th or early 20th century down to the present day, liberalism has been progressively oriented toward psychology and therapeutic technique. But advanced liberalism in the 21st century is as materialist a creed as classical liberalism was in the nineteenth, and liberal psychology remains as firmly grounded in a materialist philosophy as in Jeremy Bentham's day. As Patrick Deneen observed in a recently published and widely discussed book (*Why Liberalism Failed*), when we speak of radicals, liberals, and conservatives in their present context, we are actually referring to radical liberals, liberals, and conservative liberals, and have been for a century at least. We are speaking, then, of philosophically radical materialists, philosophically liberal materialists, and philosophically conservative ones; of Social Democratic materialists, Christian Democratic materialists, Labour materialists, Tory materialists, neoliberal materialists, Democratic materialists, and Republican materialists. So it is natural that all of these parties should have a materialist understanding of the phenomenon they call "populism" in America and in western and eastern Europe, which they condemn as the reaction by the ignorant middle and unwashed lower middle classes to what they perceive as the damaging consequences of the neoliberal economic system founded on economic competition, free trade, the globalized economy, open borders, and free migration of peoples, all undergirded by the enforced principles of multiculturalism and secularism within a global association of withering national sovereignties and societies. Today's "populist" leaders— Donald Trump, Nigel Farage, Marine Le Pen, Victor Orbàn, Sebastien Kurz (the former Chancellor) in Austria, Mario Salvini and Georgia Meloni of Italy, and Éric Zemmour in France—understand the radical incompleteness of this point of view and see the blindness of people who hold it. It is in this respect that Trump was least a Republican president—least, in fact, a Republican at all compared with his political colleagues on the right side of the aisle. It is true that he campaigned, and directed his administration, against free trade deals, the transfer of American jobs overseas, the free and unlimited importation of cheap labor known as immigration, the unemployment resulting from these things and from over-regulation, and the rest of it; still, he has always been carefully attuned to the non-economic aspect of his supporters' dissatisfaction and angst. What Republican politician of the pre-Trump era, what Republican politician even today, would have insisted that "We're all saying 'Merry Christmas' now, aren't we"?

It is for this reason that Trump's famous promise to "Make America Great Again!" has been widely, or partly, misunderstood by the man's political friends, his enemies, and people resolved to make the best of this presidency (meaning, often enough, to turn it to their selfish advantage and exploit the President himself). It is not at all clear, for instance, that the Claremont Institute's National Greatness agenda fully or accurately represents Trump's vision of America, and that of his less learned and intellectually sophisticated supporters. In February of 2017 Claremont's chairman of the board suggested that "Many Claremonters have the ear of this administration and may help Trump take what he feels in his gut and migrate it to his head." Eight months later, the president of the institute, in an address critical of the American Enterprise Institute's internationalist bent and agenda, asserted that, "we have a more urgent task at home. We have over the last hundred years been heading down the slippery slope of despotism—even if an often benign and administrative despotism."

This of course is both true and truly stated, and Claremont's insistence on "America First!" is a worthy thing. Nevertheless there is a very real and healthy difference between nationalism and patriotism, and the Institute seems inclined toward the first of these. In Donald Trump's first year in office he showed himself to be both a nationalist *and* a patriot. The two things are not mutually contradictory, yet in combination the active element of the pair tends readily to dominate the passive one, as active things will. Trump is a man of action, with an active, impetuous, and often reckless personality very similar in some ways to Theodore Roosevelt's, minus Roosevelt's formal intellect and formidable literary talent. Trump is, as Roosevelt was, a man who cares neither to be left alone, nor to leave others alone. Yet—and this estimate is based on individual impression—the mood of the portion of the country that elected him and voted for him again four years later seems to have been isolationist in a loose informal way, not simply with respect to foreign powers, but to government at every level: international, federal, state, and local. Trump's constituency seems interested above all in preventing governmental and financial officials from subjugating them, regulators from harassing, oppressing, and fencing them in—and then in being left alone. They have never been eager to restore America to international hegemony, especially not at the price hegemony demands. (The Populist Party of the late 19th and early 20th century had no interest in empire.) They *do*, however, wish their country to be respected internationally (as the popular uproar following President Biden's disastrous retreat from Afghanistan showed), but on her own terms and not in response to blackmail in the shape of demands for international aid, for armed intervention to prop up some incompetent or corrupt government on behalf of world peace, or otherwise to rescue a world in which the outhouse countries predominate from itself. Hence the shouting, the signs, and the banners at every Trump rally on behalf of MAKE AMERICA GREAT AGAIN. The same may be said of the Britons who voted for Brexit in another "populist" coup (as liberals view it) that, rumor among Remainers has it, was aided, inspired, and abetted by the Kremlin to weaken Great Britain and sabotage the European Union; the notable difference being that in the case of Brexit demonstrations on behalf of bidding the EU fare-thee-well did not occur beneath waving placards lettered MAKE THE UK GREAT AGAIN. Simple British sovereignty has always been entirely sufficient for the supporters of the Leave campaign.

All things considered however, the bedrock of populist—of popular—discontent lies deeper, and stretches far more extensively, than concerns about national pride, national sovereignty, and economic distress. It is considerably more basic, and profoundly more human, than that. It has to do with the perpetual unsettledness of everything today: of politics, culture, religion, geographical place, and demography; of grounding assurances and beliefs, including (as Lance Morrow wrote in a column for the *Wall Street Journal* in November of 2021) borders, those between nations, the sexes, or anything else. Human beings are constitutionally incapable of feeling secure and comfortable in modern liberal societies—societies mobilized by liberalism in an endless unwinnable war against the political and social evils endlessly identified by liberals and by liberal government that amount to a state of permanent revolution, of relentless and accelerating economic, social, intellectual, and technological change, whose predicate and ultimate aim are the reinvention of human nature and the redesign of human society. The manifold results of this effort—personal uncertainty, apprehension, social restlessness, agitation, and commotion—add momentum to the project along its hurtling postmodern trajectory away from the human condition of the ages and toward an unknown and unknowable future.

The liberal attitude toward the past is manifest in the contemporary liberal idea of what was once called a liberal education. The English philosopher Michael Oakeshott described "education in its most general significance…as a specific transaction which may go on between the generations of human beings in which newcomers to the scene are initiated into the world they inhabit." Oakeshott called this "a moral obligation…upon which a recognizably human life depends for its continuance." But today, liberal education is no more—or rather, it is all too recognizably *liberal*. "[D]uring the past century," Frank Furedi has noted ("No Patrimony," *First Things*, February 2018) "this natural process has been stymied. Western societies have found it increasingly difficult to socialize young people into the values of the previous generations. In the face of extraordinary technological and social change, older generations have lost confidence in the values into which they were acculturated. As things now stand, Western society is estranged from the values that inspired it in the past. It no longer provides adults with a compelling narrative for socialization," while prosecuting its "silent crusade" against its own past.

Aviezer Tucker of the Center for Russian and Eurasian Studies at Harvard, writing in the *American Interest* (January February 2017), deplored the "noxiousness" of populism, its "vulgar and vile" politicians, and suggested means by which populism itself can be suppressed and made impossible. Among them are regulating the internet to "block disinformation," avoiding referenda and plebiscites, insulating international institutions from the voters, and translating political debates into technical ones managed and determined by technocrats for the purpose of "facilitating trade and migration to stimulate the global economy and generate growth that can shorten and moderate the severity of recessions" that produce "a vicious cycle of economic decline, breakdown of trade, economic and political hostilities, and isolation[ism]"—in other words, "populism."

Karl Polanyi, the Viennese-born left-wing social democrat, journalist, and author of *The Great Transformation,* believed that the collapse of market economics and the liberal free-trade system of the 19th century that had "disembedded" economics from the larger social context in which it had been historically subsumed was directly responsible for outbreak of the Great War in 1914, and for the rise of fascism in the 1930s after that system, briefly resurrected in the 1920s, collapsed again beneath the weight of its inherent contradictions. "From the point of view of the community as a whole," Polanyi thought, "socialism is merely the continuation of that endeavor to make society a distinctively human relationship of persons which in Europe was always associated with Christian conditions." In his analysis, the state of markets determined the part fascism played in the post-war period. "In the period 1924–29, when the restoration of the market system seemed ensured, fascism faded out as a political force altogether. After 1930 the market economy was in a general crisis. Within a few years fascism was a world power."

The wider point should be obvious, and it has a plain lesson for the present time. The free-market, free-trade system which subsumes all of human society, indeed all of human life, to the economic sphere is inhuman, inhumane, humanly intolerable, and finally unworkable; eventually, society as a whole is certain to rebel against it. In the 1930s, the rebellion took the form of fascism. Today, the rebel movement is the thing neoliberals inaccurately and misleadingly call "populism." This is emphatically *not* to say that "populism" is the same thing as fascism, though liberals insist that it is. Yet the fact that they perceive an equivalence between the two shows that they are able to glimpse the similarity of their historical origins dimly, while failing to recognize the "populism" of today for what it really is.

5. Give Us Happiness, Not Greatness

In the early years of the Republic, Americans focused their efforts on democratic government, geographic expansion and settlement, and a program of national improvements intended to promote them. In the decades immediately following the War Between the States they concentrated on industrializing and amassing national wealth. Then, in the 1880s and 90s, they began to cultivate the ambition to become a dominant power in the world, a colossus benignly robed in the spotless garments of virginal democracy. Theodore Roosevelt laid the theoretical, rhetorical, and military foundations of "national greatness" that Woodrow Wilson transformed into full-blown ideological democratism as the moral justification (and *cache-sexe*) of the new republican giant. In the 1930s, the obsession with national greatness was diminished by concerns for economic survival, eclipsed during World War II by the imperative to defeat the Axis powers, and replaced between 1945 and 1991 by the alternate idea of America as "the leader of the Free World."

But immediately following the demise of the Soviet Union the neoconservative cabal resurrected "national greatness" as "national greatness conservatism," a reformulation of the ideological slogan of historical memory whose stamina was demonstrated in the presidential campaign of 2016 by the leading candidates of the two principal parties as they traded rhetorical blows and parried for advantage in a surrealistic campaign that would have delighted the heart of H.L. Mencken as the *ne plus ultra* in American politics. From the starting bell Donald Trump shouted his intention to "make America great again" and Mrs. Clinton countered by insisting that "America has never stopped being great"; an implied rebuke to her opponent's historical understanding, or his patriotism, or both. Trump of course, and some of his supporters perhaps, shrewdly perceived that if America is not great then neither are the Clintons and the Obamas and the Bushes and the federal bureaucratic monstrosity and the American military over which they preside in imperial power and splendor. The American elite, the great tortoise that aspires to bear along a more or less docile and compliant world on its heavily armored back, is determined to create and sustain a country worthy of its own greatness, as it sees it. But the great and powerful are not the whole of America but only a tiny part of it and not the best part at that but arguably the worst, the greediest, the most corrupt, the most ruthless elements of a population comprising 320 million people. They are a kakistocracy that has emerged over the past hundred years and grown in power and numbers until today, when it holds the nation in a species of

benign bondage to itself, a high-tech post-capitalist fiefdom encompass-
ing 50 states. This is the reward national greatness bestows on the American ruling class. But what benefits does it provide the other 99 percent
of the country? The answer is: none at all. America may be the richest
and most powerful nation in the world, but in terms of comfort, wealth,
health, education, security, political honesty, and public efficiency, it provides the great mass of its citizens with no more than so-called secondary
powers like Britain, France, Germany, Canada, and Australia offer theirs,
and in some instances less.

National greatness is a trick on the American public, the unsophis-
ticated lower-middle class portion of it especially. This has been evident
at least since the 1960s, when the loudest and most aggressive defenders
of the flag, an interventionist foreign policy, and President Nixon were
the hard-hats eager to match violence with violence in confronting the
crowds of anti-war demonstrators, most of them affluent college students
beguiled by vulgar Marxism. I thought at the time, and think today, that
bellicose nationalism in America is the visceral unthinking response of
uneducated and socially undistinguished people whose sense of superiority, such as it is, depends upon their status as citizens of the world's
richest and most powerful empire. No college professor, medical doctor,
or other professional much cares or thinks about whether his country is
"number one" and neither does the hedge fund manager or the stock job-
ber, except so far as national primacy maintains the dollar as the world's
exchange currency and gives him privileged access to global markets. But
the construction worker and the long-haul teamster are conscious of a
sense of self-reflected glory, and it is to these people that Trump and
Mrs. Clinton, like almost every other politician in election season, wished
to appeal. (Two notable exceptions, Barack Obama and Senator Sanders,
deserve to be respected for that.)

There is a type of disordered personality (the kind that ordinarily runs
for president) that can only be happy and satisfied in thinking that the
fate of his country, even the world, rests in its hands; and although even
in the nuclear age this belief is part of a generalized delusion of grandeur,
persons of this sort very well understand how to parley that delusion into
immense fortunes, which are not illusory at all. (The Clintons are the
supreme example today of such people.) Yet their power and their money

have no peculiarly national quality about them, and the greatness these people flatter themselves they possess is neither a culturally specific American greatness nor reward for a patriotism that would make its acquisition almost a matter of absence of mind, like the British Empire. A striking example was the panicked reaction of the so-called Republican "establishment" to the electoral success of Donald Trump, a response having nothing to do with "Our Principles" (the GOP, like the Democracy, has no principles whatsoever except to win at any cost) but exclusively with their subsidized lunches at the Capitol Grill, their lavish campaign donations, their power and influence as office holders and political fixers, their perquisites, their celebrity, and their easy money. None of it had anything to do with their noisily affirmed purpose of "keeping America great," as their continuing determination since 2016 to export jobs and manufacturing plants and import Third World immigrants on the dole and potential jihadists shows. Whether Donald Trump, campaigning on a platform to keep jobs in America and (illegal) immigrants out, was functionally a part of the establishment's national greatness scam or a joyful saboteur of it was uncertain until after his inauguration. In his four years in office that followed, he won his spurs and proved his bona fides.

Early in the last century, "American greatness" meant joining the ranks of the world's great powers and preaching the gospel of democracy to our little brown and yellow brothers in oppressive tropical climes full of heathenism, malaria, and poisonous creatures, among them leftist guerillas. After 1945, it meant defending America from Communism and winning the Cold War. But since the early 1990s it has meant asserting and maintaining America's status as sole superpower and imposing "American values"—by propaganda where possible, by military force when necessary—on a benighted but resistant world, a world in which America's will must be made irresistible and her word law. The power and other advantages this policy confers on the various departments—political, military, financial, corporate, legal, charitable, and managerial—of our ruling class are perfectly obvious. The burdens and liabilities imposed by the "strenuous life" advocated by the American elite upon ordinary citizens are equally plain.

Global domination by whatever name, empire or hegemony, depends upon a strong military force engaged in perennial combat around the world. Since Washington ended the draft in the 1970s, the rank and file—and above it—of the American military has been drawn mostly from the lower middle class political commentators call "populist," much of it lacking a high school degree and the larger part without education beyond that level. It is people of this class who do the fighting and the bleeding and the dying in hopeless slum-countries like Iraq and Somalia, where dwell lesser yet supposedly educable peoples without the law, and who feature as pathetic human wrecks in advertisements for Wounded Warriors on the nightly Fox News shows. It is true that many American soldiers are recruited from the ethnic pools of natural warriors described by David Hackett Fischer in *Albion's Seed,* and for whom military life provides both employment and the opportunity to develop and exercise the instincts and talents scorned by their social and intellectual betters, but only for so long as the work lasts—into middle age if they are fortunate—after which life is too often a pieced-together affair lasting until early retirement on military pension. Any broadly liberal government might be expected to consider this a scandalous waste of human potential—but not the government that has reigned in Washington for decades now and is presently fighting to preserve its privileged future from the grasping hands of the native barbarians.

World domination and intervention, the humanitarian as well as the political and military sort, cost money as well as lives, and financial expenditures abroad are inevitably matched by confiscatory levels of taxation or unmanageable national deficits certain to end in ruinous taxes and ultimately in national financial collapse—or both. Here again the burden is borne by the general run of the public, while the national greatness class can count not just on saving its own skin but on conjuring national catastrophe into personal financial and political profit. Congress can pass all the legislation it can think up to "stop loopholes" and in other ways create the legal and financial "level playing field" it is always talking about and promising to establish—and still the financial, legal, and political elites will find ways to circumvent and exploit each and every one of them. No law was ever written that could not be got round by clever and powerful people and their legal guns; one might say that the unspoken purpose of the laws in an unashamedly plutocratic society like our own is to spin bright veils of bogus fairness to cover the acts of legalized theft perpetrated beneath them in the smug expectation that the special interests represented by the legislators and their friends will prevail without *hoi polloi* ever becoming aware of the hoax. In America today, if you rise far enough and grow big enough, you can't ever lose—and you can't ever sink. The equivalent of the golden parachute is the monogrammed golden life jacket, and the golden life preserver that goes with it.

But beyond the military and tax burdens one may discern more subtle and extensive ills incurred by the fatal obsession with "national greatness." One of them is the hyper-politicization of American society that large national ambitions and projects, domestic and foreign, naturally produce. European travelers to the United States in the early 19th century noted, usually with half-amused scorn, the intense restlessness and frenetic activity of the Americans. The frenzy of the time centered on commerce and industry. Today it is mostly about politics, including the politics of industry and corporate business, but also and perhaps more importantly Washington's global involvement through military intervention and support, foreign aid, globalist economics, immigration, migration—and now terrorism, which is substantially a reaction to America's long history of intervention in the Middle East, Central Asia, and in Africa. No government that insists as ours does on great and intrusive national ambitions and projects at home and abroad can avoid meddlesomeness, and governmental meddlesomeness in a democracy invariably produces restlessness and quarrelsomeness as society becomes less democratic and more managed, more socially and politically "aware" as liberals say and less concentrated on individual business interests and personal concerns. The government that provokes bitter controversy, dissension, and uncertainty by its American greatness policies abroad is the same government that believes America can never be great until she has established a domestic society upon the explicit repudiation of the laws of nature, of human nature, and of God's nature. In America today no one can feel at peace—with the world, with his country, with his neighbors, with his family, or with himself—and a disturbed, angry, anxious, and increasingly fearful people can never be a happy people except (perhaps) at the highest levels of society, which thrive on endemic restlessness, insatiable ambition, unflagging activity and excitement, and constant strife—the strenuous life. Where Donald Trump fitted into all this was impossible to tell until January 20, 2017. His keen sense of the deep American *angst* and its origins explains his remarkable success as president, just as the persistent loyalty of his electoral base and his still massive popularity as registered in the polls are the most dramatic manifestations of Americans' confusion and unhappiness, with the possible exception of the massacres in the schools and the riots in the streets.

From the beginning, Donald Trump has had great appeal not only for the lower middle "populist" class but for a broad section of the American middle class as well; people who, like the "populists," respond enthusiastically—and gratefully—to his plain speaking and his refusals to genuflect, apologize, and explain himself to the increasingly hated political class he defies, and who despise him in return. Plain speaking had been out of fashion with American politicians, Republican and Democratic, liberal and conservative, since the presidency of Harry Truman when they pretended at least to admire the Missourian's haberdasherly bluntness. Unfortunately, Trump's repeated promise on the campaign trail and as president to make America great again is actually the least plain element of his famous style. The plainest, most direct, and most welcome thing Trump (or any president) could ever promise Americans is to promise to make America happy again, happy as she has not been for many a decade—and the hell with greatness, like spinach.

6. The End of the Free World

The Soviet Union and the Soviet Empire have been gone for more than 30 years, but still American internationalists, Democrats and Republicans alike, persist in speaking of the "Free World," quite as if Earth continues to be divided between the liberal-democratic-capitalist and the communist camps. This "Free World" talk persisted throughout President Trump's inauguration, all of it aimed at promoting the belief that the President was not just letting the "Free World" down but turning his back on it, careless of whether it survived, languished, or perished without American military and financial aid and diplomatic support. No one, right or left, ever thinks to ask whether the "Free World" still exists in a sense in which the term has any meaning at all.

From the start, the "Free World" was an ideological concept and thus an aggressive one. Its rhetorical nemesis was the "communist bloc," a world that was "un-free" in a specific ideological and totalitarian way on the far side of the Iron Curtain. For champions of the "Free World," the Un-free World did not ordinarily include, for ideological and political purposes, countries whose political and social traditions were traditional and pre-democratic—empires, monarchies, even old-fashioned, non-ideological dictatorships with which the "Free World" was willing to make alliances and do business as part of its strategy against the un-Free World. For the "Free World," the un-Free World meant the Marxist-Communist one, a mortal enemy so great that the world itself was too small to make settled coexistence possible. ("There's room for only one of us in this town.") It is true that American liberals were more or less overtly hostile to imperialism and authoritarianism in every form, and that after World War II they were quick to turn on their former European allies—the British especially—by encouraging and even forcing the dismemberment of their colonial empires. Still, Washington in the post-war era continued to operate on the assumption that whatever was not communist was more or less on the side of the angels—and of the greatest of the archangels, America herself. Today, as American internationalists of both parties fight to keep the Cold War alive (an effort made incalcuably easier by Putin's renewal of it in Ukraine) and even to chill it still further, one may reasonably question, first, their assumption that anything properly describable as the "Free World" persists in the 21st century, and second, whether the United States is morally qualified to lead or even to speak for it—if it does.

The matter depends to a considerable extent upon whether one believes the United States to be still a free country herself in the historical sense, and the "Free World," whose symbolic leader remains the U.S., similarly free. According to reports issuing regularly from fervently democratist sources like the State Department, various Washington agencies, and an array of NGOs, the answer is a qualified "yes:" free, though of course never free enough. Current popular movements across the United States and Europe pejoratively identified by liberal establishments as "populist"—in America that undefined thing called Trumpism, in England Brexitism, in France *Le Penisme*, in Holland the Party for Freedom, in Italy the Five-Star movement, in Germany the Alternative for Germany, in Hungary Jobbik, and so on—indicate the opposite. The new popul(arist) opposition to Western establishmentarianism thinks of itself as a principled democratic remnant of a world that was indeed once free, but is becoming less free every day under the thumb of a political, social, and cultural establishment dedicated to an Orwellian ideology bent on imposing soft tyranny in the name of freedom. For "populists", the "Free World" is not just an evil parody of the old Western world but an unreal one built on the lies and the self-serving illusions of a *faux* elite. Certain people whose business or interest it is to consider such things argue that communism was defeated in Eastern Europe and Western Asia only to reestablish itself in Western Europe and North America.

The primary threat to freedom in the Western countries is advanced liberal culture, liberal government as shaped by that culture being oddly secondary. Great as the power of government over modern society has become, popular opinion has been shaping politics to greater extent than governments have been, as recent studies of partisan political alignment in the United States suggest. In this sense the people really do have the government they deserve, or at least half of it does. But while the American and the British electorates divide nearly equally between liberals and anti-liberals, liberalism has plainly become the official culture throughout the West, the culture of the elites and the governments they staff and control. Just as plainly, this culture is anti-democratic, as well as liberal: overbearing, controlling, intolerant, and with obvious totalitarian instincts. All ideologically motivated governments and societies are evil, since their ideological formation rests on a foundation of metaphysical falsity. Falsity by definition is untruth; and just as "the truth shall set you free," so untruth will make you un-free—indeed, it will make you a slave. Advanced liberalism, having fashioned an alternative metaphysical reality for the world, is working to impose its intellectual creation on reality, which can be effectively (though temporarily) resisted solely by brute force and the curtailment of basic freedoms; a business well under way across the United States and the West as liberal governments insist, with growing impatience and renewed determination, that their people must deny Christian truth and God's law and renounce the natural human instincts, affirmations, sentiments, and loyalties on which personal and social identity, security, contentment, and human happiness depend, while affirming the liberal creed of materialism, universal brotherhood, and moral relativity.

So for the past third of a century or so the liberal culture of the "Free World" has concentrated on making that world less free. Simultaneously, the American government has summoned its Western allies, in the name of "freedom" and "democracy," to extend and impose the new American version of both beyond the Western world and to enforce them with all its military might and the enthusiastic support of the new liberal culture at home. It is hard to say which of the two is worse. The American civic culture wants, in addition to free and democratically elected government everywhere, liberal-capitalist-global economies, permeable if not open borders, social equality and the denial of sexual differences between the sexes, religious equality and secularism, sexual hedonism, easy access to contraception and abortion, and the recognition of gay rights, up to and including gay marriage. American popular culture brings synthetic vulgarity on the commercial scale, moral relativity and immorality in the "arts," cheap American-style clothing mass-produced for the masses, and the obliteration of local cuisines by junk food sold from American franchises. Civic and popular culture merge in the relentless politicization of Hollywood and of the American and other Western media, which conscientiously infuse their productions with progressive "messages" carefully shaped to promote social inclusiveness, feminism, sodomy, and resentment of supposedly greedy businessmen and corporations working to impoverish the poor, corrupt governments, thwart "democracy," and destroy "the environment." Lacking the communist monster to slay, the "Free World" has replaced it with the avowed enemy of "our core values and principles," capable of assuming a thousand different forms but readily identifiable by the absence from its forehead of the Great Seal of Approval with which Washington marks its own: the "un-American."

Sergey Kislyak, the notorious Russian ambassador to the United States at the time of Trump's election and inauguration, once reminded an American audience that, "we don't impose our exceptionalism on you." His remark went largely unnoted by the media (or anyone else), of course. The ambassador, a cultivated and sophisticated cosmopolitan, is surely conscious of the irony inherent in the fact that the United States, having hoped for decades to rescue the Soviet peoples from the tyranny of Marxist-Leninism, is presently attempting to subject the Russians to the tyranny of American liberalism that in its newest form is a direct descendant of Marxist-Leninism. It may also have occurred to Mr. Kislyak, who has a close familiarity with and knowledge of the United States, that not only does the "Free World" no longer exist but that, if it does, Washington has no business leading it. (Some years ago James P. Rubin, the Democratic operative, annointed Angela Merkel, the German chancellor, as the new "Leader of the Free World" and the old liberal order. If so, she—and the country she betrayed by inviting over a million largely Muslim "refugees" into it—are welcome to that honor.)

Writing in the Winter 2017 number of *Modern Age*, David Hein showed how post-war history might have been different. In an excellent essay, "The Marshall Plan," he argued that the European Recovery Program (to which the name of the then-Secretary of State George C. Marshall was attached), though more readily remembered today as another misguided exercise in liberal humanitarianism and idealism (which is how conservatives of that day saw it), was in fact an example of "conservative reform as a weapon of war" and thus wholly consistent with the conservative foreign policy of the Truman administration that stood in stark contrast with its liberal domestic program. "The Truman containment strategy," Hein wrote, "incorporated a deliberate rejection of Wilsonian universalism in favor of—in the words of diplomatic historian John Lewis Gaddis—'independent centers of power, in which nations subject to Soviet pressure would have both the means and the will to resist it themselves.' Gaddis notes that for George F. Kennan, director of the State Department's policy planning staff, 'what was required was not to remake the world in the image of the United States, but rather to preserve its diversity against attempts to remake it in the image of others.'" Kennan, in Hein's view, understood containment as a matter of reducing rather than of enlarging America's global ambitions, while strengthening her allies and hewing to the balance of power that prevailed throughout the international system. Kennan's favored policy was therefore congruent with Russell Kirk's belief that "the diversity of economic and political institutions throughout the world" should be accepted by Washington. "Soviet hegemony ought not to be succeeded by American hegemony,"

Kirk thought, and American conservatives, while working on behalf of "the defense of order and justice and freedom," should press for a "conservative foreign policy" that was above all prudent, rather than interventionist or isolationist.

The United States today is less the symbol of the "Free World" than of the globalist one she created by spreading a false idea of freedom internationally, after imposing it at home. Having recognized in Vladimir Putin a significant obstacle to realizing their ambitions decades before he invaded Ukraine, hyper-imperialists like John Bolton do not seem averse to taking advantage of Putin's attacks in Ukraine to revive the Cold War they thought they had won once and for all more than a quarter of a century ago. They were close to succeeding in their ambition before the first months of Donald Trump's administration, when foreign governments were compelled to accept the fact that the new President had no interest in nation-building, championing and protecting "human rights," propping up the United Nations, and assisting other vital internationalist projects being promoted by the former leaders of the "Free World." Small wonder that the Deep State (and plenty of others) loathed and feared him and did their level best (as we know today) to sabotage his administration and lay the man himself low.

CHAPTER FOUR | SCIENCE AND DEMOCRACY

A virtue of America's quadrennial election cycle is its success in revealing and giving form to whatever popular malaise has set in over the past four years, whether the results of the elections themselves address the disorder or not, and occasionally in raising real issues, even if only by implication. In this respect, the presidential elections of 2016 and 2020 were more significant than previous ones going back many years had been.

1. Power in the Post-Modern World

No one doubts the depth and breadth of popular discontent in this country, which appears to be attaining critical mass. Democrats put this down during President Obama's time in office to Congress's stonewalling the White House by refusing to act on legislation Democrats wanted passed and to economic inequality, Republicans to the Democrats' determination to transform America morally, socially, and demographically and to Obama's caesarism in resorting to executive action when he found himself thwarted politically. Both parties agreed that the electorate's enthusiasm for presidential candidates from beyond the circle of professional politicians, like Donald Trump, Ben Carson, and Carly Fiorina on the Republican side, and maverick politicians like Senator Sanders and Elizabeth Warren on the Democratic one, signaled the voters' lack of trust in their incumbent representatives personally and the political establishment in general.

This explanation, while true so far as it went, failed to account for the unease, suspicion, frustration, genuine anger, and behind these the dim fearfulness of the American public. ("Outsiders," of course, are hardly unknown in American political history. The young Republic honored the ideal of the citizen farmer and the citizen legislator, and *Mr. Smith Goes to Washington* was not meant to be understood as a political thriller or horror story. Barack Obama was "an outsider.") It is the kind of fear produced by the smell of danger without danger's outlines coming into sight, the sense of a threat unidentified. The pollsters reported then, as they do now, that Americans believe their country is in decline, her best years behind her. Economic insecurity and moral confusion in a relativistic age contribute to this impression. So does an awareness of civic impotence that is part of the concern with the perceived untrustworthiness of the political class—its fundamental dishonesty and the betrayal of the public by men and women in control of every major American institution whose democratic pretense to "transparency" and "accountability" only points out their determination to use their power and influence to have their own way with the country, come hell or high water.

The most significant accomplishment in the history of Western civilization is not the creation of free institutions, representative government, and democracy. It is not the rise of a capitalist economy and the free market. It is not the establishment of free inquiry and the discoveries of modern science credited with leading Europeans out of the age of blind superstition, ignorance, and enslavement by nature and by priests. It is not the sequence of causal events in economics and technology that produced the Industrial Revolution and the materialist revolution, the explosion of affluence and of human physical well-being industrialism made possible. It is the creation of Power over two millennia as a response to the impulse St. Augustine called the *libido dominandi*—the lust for Power for its own sake, for domination and control, valued by moderns even above its innumerable practical uses and benefits.

Power in this sense—collective, diffuse, impersonal, and omnipresent, settling like a fog over every institution, every area of human activity, every social association, and coming to rest finally upon thought itself—is a phenomenon of the modern West and increasingly the whole of the modern world. Power and the relationships of power are as old as humanity itself, but power in the sense of the traditional idea of the thing is something very different from Power in its contemporary meaning. When we speak of Nebuchadnezzer as having had power, or Caesar, or Charlemagne, or Henry VIII, or Robespierre, we mean personal power wielded in societies based on the concept and fact of personal power operating among rival personalities and groups, and valued indeed for its *being* personal—limited to the personal reach of the powerful and their circle. Power of the personal sort exists today, of course, and always will. But in the modern industrial and post-industrial world, personal power, even at the apex of power, is—despite ceremonial appearances—almost unidentifiable among the vast impersonal and largely unaccountable powers inherent in modern and post-modern political, bureaucratic, administrative, economic, legal, educational, scientific, and social institutions. Though the leader of a nuclear-armed country may choose to incinerate the world at the touch of a button, the power to do so does not reside in his capacity as a particular man but in a convergence of institutional powers that finally constrains personal power to two potentially unimaginably catastrophic choices—wholly unlike the regal authority that dispatched an English army, led by Henry V himself, across the Channel to engage the French at Agincourt six centuries ago. The ultimate power of the man in the Oval Office or the Kremlin is one no morally sane person would relish in the crisis—he might even regret having sought it in the first place—but the Power that created the hydrogen bomb is something Western man deliberately willed for himself. It is the ultimate example of personal power—authority displaced by Power.

The modern world rests on science and democracy, but the two things are essentially incompatible. Science is knowledge, as Francis Bacon said, and democracy is said to be freedom. Yet people are not equally capable of knowledge, something naturally reserved to the few, while Western science is unimaginably powerful—hence undemocratic. A regime, in the Greek sense of the word, that is dominated by science is necessarily a regime created and governed by elites. But Americans want the benefits of modern science *and* 18th century republican freedoms, and the newly made-over Republican Party today demands them. It is obvious that they, and we, cannot have both. Liberalism and communism have always assumed that the two goods could be reconciled (though neither today understands freedom by in the 18th century meaning of the word) by state planning and state ownership of production. But communist regimes have ended in political, economic, cultural, and human catastrophe, and liberal ones are going in the same direction, though so far less brutally.

The Western project since the Renaissance has been to "vex" nature, as Bacon put it, in order to understand her, and to understand her in order to harness her in the service of men. What had been the primary purpose of "philosophy," to study God's works as a means of apprehending and giving greater glory to Him, became secondary as modern science advanced, until early by the 18th century it had been abandoned entirely. Since then the goal of science has been the domination and control of nature for the purpose of exploiting her. That aim has been realized far beyond Bacon's wildest possible imaginings, and even those of 19th and early 20th century scientists. According to Scripture, the world was made for man to work and develop by the sweat of his brow. It is only right and just that men should bind nature hand and foot to answer their needs. But as God faded as a presence from behind scientific investigation and enterprise, man took His place in his self-estimation and in his own ambition, which aspired increasingly to a power that would rival divine omnipotence and make God irrelevant.

Power means control, and man's power over nature implies man's power over men as well. Before Power stepped in between nature and man, men were ruled chiefly by the powers of nature; since that time they have been ruled chiefly by men and the works of men, more so all the time. This is partly from necessity but also because scientifically minded people, people who like to control things, like also to control people, where there is a need for such control and where there isn't.

In the second half of the 19th century the new and unprecedentedly powerful industrial civilization that was revolutionizing Western societies provoked a counter-revolution on both the right and the left that aimed to control and direct industrial capitalism by political action designed to address industrialism's social, economic, environmental, and political consequences. This counter-revolution had only limited success, but in that era the effort to tame the mechanical Leviathan seemed feasible, providing reformers with a sense of assurance and confidence in a still manageable world. A century and a half later the post-industrial world, having become unintelligible to most people in theory and in practice, and seemingly uncontrollable by the private entrepreneurs who own and operate it and the governmental functionaries attempting to regulate it, offers scant cause for similar confidence. The artificial world man has created for himself has achieved an extent and an opaque complexity that rival, in their unintelligibility, the natural world before Western science began to investigate it. This has provoked in post-industrial men a fear and apprehension analogous to the primeval human fear of nature primeval. Yet neither the science nor the political system that could rescue them from the state of post-nature is evident anywhere.

Modern science has created a world difficult for most people to fathom, and too complex for politicians and administrators to manage, assuming they themselves understand it—a very questionable assumption. Unbridled advancement in scientific technique and the mass democracy technology has helped make possible simply do not agree with each other.

Science and the fruits of science, technology and its political, economic, social, and environment consequences, are more easily and conveniently managed, without popular intrusion, by administrators than by politicians. Owing to this, and to the vast bureaucratic apparatus set in place by advanced liberal states, Western political systems are being steadily depoliticized and deprived of the means of self-control by the loss of the capacity for political action, in the United States as in the European Union, where the subject has been a major issue for intellectual and political debate for some time now. Of all power's forms, diffuse power is the hardest to resist, making resistance seem hopeless to frustrated and angry citizens. Critics who deplore the "polarization" of American political life fail to see what is actually going on: The anti-establishmentarian wing of the GOP is seeking to *re-politicize* American politics against the wishes of the Democratic-Republicans (or Social Republicans) and the Democratic Party, all of whom are more than happy with a system dominated and directed by administrators, lawyers, and judges and in which executive power is exercised when and where needed to correct democratic political action, or fill in for it. John Boehner, the former Republican speaker of the House of Representatives who pushed "comprehensive immigration reform" for years, was not merely relieved by President Obama's executive action granting amnesty to more than a million illegal aliens that Congress had refused to pass on numerous occasions; he was reported to have encouraged it by an advance promise to the President not to oppose the flagrantly unconstitutional order Obama had for years protested he was constitutionally prohibited from issuing.

People running for political office either have confidence in their ability to operate effectively in an increasingly incomprehensible and un-controllable world, a world of Power diffused across hundreds or even thousands of administrative institutions and agencies staffed by bureau-crats, or they are able to manage a convincing show of confidence. Many, in any event, care little or nothing about accomplishing anything of sig-nificance so long as they can enjoy the powers and perquisites of office—as is probably the case with the majority of office seekers. The voters they hope to convince aren't so confident. Indeed, they have pretty much de-cided to ignore the claims and pretensions of the professional politicos. The preference of today's electorate for candidates with no political expe-rience is analogous to the eagerness of the big commercial publishers for "debut" novelists who, lacking a track record, can be touted before publi-cation date as blooming geniuses and potential best-selling authors. It also reflects Americans' misapprehension of the contemporary political system. Where Power is impersonalized by institutions and regulations and where personal authority is largely absent, politics is reduced to show business—the smoke and mirrors routine at which Barack Obama excelled through-out his career—and illegal fiat, also a specialty of the 44th President.

Where the rule of bureaucracy prevails in a society over-developed in almost every respect to the point where it is swamped by problems and confusions undreamt of by previous generations down to the last two or three, that society becomes unmanageable and its impatient and angry cit-izens increasingly ungovernable—an accurate description of the Western nations in the 21st century. In these circumstances it is probably of little real importance which political candidates Americans elect to office, so long they aren't Caligulas, Lincolns, and Stalins, since, whoever they are, they are certain to find themselves submerged in their intractable, incom-prehensible, and impossible jobs, as the rest of us are being submerged in the New Creation of our own making.

2. The Anti-Prometheans

Whether Barack Obama ever spoke the sentence himself, the words "We are the ones we've been waiting for" have come to stand as the motto of his presidency. In the same way, "This is the one we've been waiting for" is a succinct representation of the issue of climatic change the international left has taken as its Gaia-sent pretext for a global government, or rather global governance, by the scientists and other "experts."

A review of almanacs going back a couple of centuries (the *Farmer's Almanac* was founded in 1792), national and international records, economic history, and common sense shows that the change in global climate observable today is both real and at least partly caused by the Industrial Revolution that got under way at the start of the 19th century. Industrialism was the material result of the deliberate replacement of speculative and theoretical science, known (as stated earlier) up until the 17th century or shortly before as "philosophy," by practical science in a deliberate attempt to give humanity the greatest achievable power over nature, a self-conscious intellectual project building on Sir Francis Bacon's dictum "Knowledge is power."

Industrialism itself, on the other hand, was not a concerted program but the *ad hoc* opportunistic pursuit of technique necessary to build machines of increasing utility to men and nations, their business and commercial interests and governments especially. Practical though its intentions were, the industrial system has never made natural, human, political, cultural, or even economic sense for reasons I cannot consider here but that have become increasing clear with the passage of time and the course of civilization. Clearly industrialism, seen from the Christian perspective, is sacrilegious in its conception, its development, and its results. Today we are witnessing an implicit public acknowledgement of that fact—less often by Christians, ironically, than by secularists and pagans who propose to reverse the unhealthy and destructive effects of industrialism; not by dismantling it (the left, every bit as greedy and grasping and luxury loving as the rest of us, wants to have its cake, eat it, and go on to bake many more cakes) but by using scientific expertise to adjust it and political expertise to exploit the program as a pretext and a means for achieving the power over human beings that Bacon envisioned for men over nature. Unlike the building up of the industrial system in the 19th and 20th centuries by "rugged" and fiercely competitive individuals and their companies, contemporary efforts to "save the planet" are part of a self-conscious, deeply moralistic, and well coordinated project of the global elites and the left to accomplish what international communism failed to do. Their primary aim is to rule the planet, to which "saving" it at best secondary, even incidental. The extent to which the movement, with its carefully cultivated aura of a religious crusade, has succeeded in concealing its motives while winning support for its agenda is suggested by one particular document hailed by progressives everywhere, despite its authorship by the world's most prominent Christian. That is the papal encyclical "Laudato Si'," issued from the Vatican in 2015, whose prescriptions for reversing global warming are notable chiefly for their congruity with the means advocated by the pagan experts and politicians who are running the wider show. As industrialism was developed with no broad concern for, and no thought given to, its implications for the future of the natural world, so the climatic change agenda is being pursued with no consideration for the welfare of the human environment—for political, corporate, associational, and individual freedom and autonomy, and the general principle of subsidiarity.

Beyond the political and moral objections to the Climate Crusade lie a large number of practical ones. Unfavorable or unwanted climatic change is precisely the sort of challenge that human groups—naturally rivalrous, self-regarding, self-aggrandizing, advantage-seeking, dishonest, and deceitful in their relations with one another—are least suited to address in a fair, honest, free, competent, and effective way. Uniting or consolidating these associations, more or less by force, at the international level up from the tribal one at which most of the world's people have lived for millenia, to establish "a world without nations" would only boot the problems that exist today in a national context to a higher level of human organization. The ever-upward translation of political responsibility has been liberalism's solution for individual and collective problems for almost as long as liberalism itself has existed. The liberal certainty that assigning responsibility to a higher, wider, vaguer, and less accountable authority is the answer to otherwise intractable difficulties is based on the mistaken assumption that the higher authority will be more visionary, competent, effective, disinterested, honest, and altruistic than the ones below it. History has invalidated this confidence many times over. The Industrial Revolution could not possibly have been planned in advance, as the hideous results of the effort to create almost overnight an efficient and acceptable alternative to it in the Soviet Union showed.

The same goes for socialism as a rational plan to construct a global utopia and for "socialism in one country," the project Stalin adopted for the Soviet Union after the internationalist one had collapsed.

Beyond the impossibility of an effective, honest, fair, and republican international political structure to halt or reverse climatic change are the overwhelming complexities of weather and atmospherics as natural phenomena and also those of "the science," as people say today, whose findings are not only partial but widely disputed despite the pretense of consensus the "scientific community" (politically progressive scientists) makes in order to present a common political front to the world. Though scientists seem largely agreed (or say they are) on "what we know" on the broad outlines of climatic activity, they are far from agreeing on a great many of the details, many of which are certain to be crucial in trying to control, as well as to understand, the climate. And even were climatic change sufficiently well understood in its general principles, the particular variables are far too various to be humanly comprehensible *in toto*.

Moreover, as scientists like to remind us all, science is conducted by "scientific method" that includes trial and error and a process of experimentation involving the presence of controls to offset the experiment. It is hard to see how, especially in what they warn is a fast-moving, cumulative, and critical natural process (or rather combination of processes), there could possibly be time for satisfactory experiment and for the design of adequate controls and their efficient observation. There is, of course, no adequate control available to stand in for Earth itself. Finally, beyond agreeing on what measures need to be taken to counter climatic change, we, "the world community" (liberalism recognizes what must be thousands of these largely imaginary "communities"), must be able to agree not only on what is to be done, but to whom. (Lenin would have understood.) Both these things are plainly impossible. If the government of the United States cannot balance the federal budget, if the British government has difficulty fully extracting itself (even after Brexit) from the European Union, and if the EU cannot agree on the desirability for defensible exterior borders to protect its 27 members from foreign invasion and how to establish them, it is madness to suppose that the "world community" could possibly resolve what the scientific one tells us is a global problem of unimaginable dimensions. The left is aware of this fact, of course, and no doubt many scientists are as well, despite their notorious ignorance of human nature (no matter how much psychology the psychologists and psychiatrists know) and their hopeless and oft-demonstrated political *naïveté*. But for them, it all is beside the point: Their final objective is the acquisition of a final unholy power, not a cooler planet.

Supposing human beings really do have the ability to "save the planet"—a more than dubious supposition—no attempt at any such project could be made without the global imposition of totalitarian societies using totalitarian means to forward it. This forces the question whether the human race is morally obligated to enslave itself to a global politburo of scientific and political "experts" for the purpose of preventing radical, or even catastrophic, climatic change. The question is a theological one, sure to be swept aside and ignored by secularists and other pagans as irrelevant. (They already have Pope Francis on their side, anyway.) Yet the Bible tells us that "the world was made for man." And if man chose to unmake that world, as indeed he seems to have done, it was of his own free will that he did it. And so it is just that he should suffer the natural consequences of what the German naturalist Alexander von Humboldt in the early 19th century called his "meddling"—but suffer in his intact God-given human nature, not some warped half-human one forced upon him by tyrannical powers wielding the butt end of a gun and mind control. Ecologists and environmentalists object to this argument by inviting us to consider the "innocent" animal kingdom, and even the vegetable and mineral ones. Why should these suffer extinction and destruction when *homo sapiens*, at some sacrifice to himself, can save them? But to recur to theology, the Creator and Author of life made these lower kingdoms subordinate to men. And the Apostle assures us that, "This world is passing away," to be succeeded by "a new Heaven and a new Earth." Even modern scientists, who predict that the world will end in a funeral pyre, consumed by solar fire a few billion years hence, view its destruction with equanimity. And our own destruction as well. The brain is purely an electric phenomenon, they say, not the finite material organ of an eternal spirit, and this claim too they calmly accept. What then are several billion years—or a few hundred, or a few score, or a few tens—more or less of Earth and mortal existence? Better sooner than later, perhaps, if the alternative is that men, whose souls are infinite, should be condemned to sacrifice the health and integrity of those souls on the altar of a finite and doomed world.

Still, the appeal to theology and the supernatural appears unnecessary and even beside the point when we turn from the world of science and the millenarian dreams of ambitious totalitarians to that of work-a-day politics early in the 21st century. While man-made global warming is real enough, and what globalists wish to make of it should be equally obvious to everyone, their grim and gray fortresses in the air will likely remain there for a period whose limit may be defined by an angry reaction against globalism, economic elites, and political establishments everywhere. Whatever "populism" is, and however one defines it, the "populists" themselves may be expected to resist a global mobilization of political and economic agents in a crusade to "save the planet," or anything else for that matter. They are simply not going to allow it to proceed, since to vote a lot of anti-promethean politicians out of office is a much easier job than constructing an international system aimed at stealing fire back from us mortals whom it has warmed and fed for ages, and returning it to the gods.

The electoral solution is not only the easiest, it is also the most thorough-going one to the problem of post-modern politics. Progressive, globalist politicians are anti-prometheans principally where the matter of fossil fuels are concerned. When it comes to human beings, they intend to play the role of Prometheus to the hilt by acquiring and exercising a control over their citizens as great or greater than the mastery achieved by that heedless and reckless god over nature: an ambition they have unwittingly, ineptly, and perhaps fatally revealed over the course of the Covid-19 pandemic by adopting draconian, illiberal, and wholly undemocratic measures to suppress it, including the shutdown of economies around the world, the lockdown of citizens, and the suspension of social life, an uninterrupted series of mandates that they reverse as rapidly as they announce them, only to replace these by new and equally futile ones. Worse still—if possible—they have introduced and attempted to enforce these policies in a hectoring and insultingly condescending manner that has infuriated the popular majority, whom it exhorts to "Believe the science!" while encouraging what is probably an acquiescent minority to condemn it as ignorant, anti-intellectual, and stupid, while thinking even better of itself than it had done before. The vast majority of people, in the West at least, are not anti-scientific; if anything, they are too credulous when it comes to the claims of science, and have been for two centuries. They believe in scientific method and technique, are grateful for the material benefits science has brought them, and hope and expect it will bring them still more benefits in future. And they believe too, and trust, the scientists with whom they are closely acquainted in daily life—their personal physicians, for instance. What they do *not* believe in, and with good reason as the past couple of years have demonstrated with a bitter and devastating clarity, are scientists who sign on with government and become ambitious, power-mad, and narcissistic politicians; scientists of whom the preeminent example today is Dr. Anthony Fauci in the United States, and certain of the more prominent medical men in Great Britain's socialist and grossly inefficient National Health Service.

"The science" changes with every passing moment of the day, as the results of one experiment are instantly superseded by another. Scientists like Dr. Fauci never change when they are on to something good, and intend to keep it that way.

CHAPTER FIVE | THE POLITICAL ADVANTAGES OF LIBERALISM

Everyone in America today—right, left, or middle, if there still is one—can agree that the response to Donald Trump's presidency was unprecedented in American political history. Liberals' clinically hysterical reaction to the President's plans for everything from The Wall, to the travel ban, to his response to the Charlottesville unpleasantness in 2017, to his cancellation of his predecessor's probably unconsitutional executive order permitting participants in the Deferred Action for Childhood Arrivals to remain in the country for a fixed period of time and apply for work permits here, to his policy of "zero tolerance" of illegal border crossers demonstrated that the nature of the profound disagreement between Trump and his critics was—and remains—not political, but religious.

1. The Liberal Religion

For liberals, Trumpism is heresy against what has been called the modern American civic religion, but in fact is religion pure and simple. The reaction against the reaction is nothing less than the outraged response by America's national church against dissenters from its unwritten creed. American politicians, Republican and Democratic alike, have been trying to conceal the fact from the country by their increasingly frequent and now frantic appeals to "America's core values," or more simply and inexactly "who we are"—cant phrases which upon examination reflect only the "values" that liberals of both parties have invented and tried to impose on Americans for decades. Their appeals having failed to produce the desired effect in approximately half the American population, the high priests and metaphorical pew sitters of the Church of Christ Without Christ have turned from public exhortation to public demonstrations, often violent ones, to rally the troops at the beginning of what looks more and more to be the Second American Civil War.

The Random House Dictionary of the English Language (New York, 1967) defines "Religion" as follows:

> 1.) Concern over what exists beyond the visible world, **differentiated from philosophy in that it operates through faith or intuition rather than reason** and **generally including the idea of the existence of** a single being, a group of beings, **an external principle,** or a transcendent spiritual entity that has created the world, **that governs it, that controls its destinies,** or that intervenes occasionally in the natural course of its history, **as well as the idea that ritual, prayer, spiritual exercises, certain principles of everyday conduct, etc., are expedient, due, or spiritually rewarding, or arise naturally out of an inner need as a human response to the belief in such a being, principle, etc.**

The boldface parts of this paragraph indicate those aspects of religious belief that modern, or advanced, liberalism shares with other religions. Taking these correspondences more or less in order, one notes that modern liberalism, excessively rational and even rationalistic in its classical phase, in embracing three basic axioms—the uniformity of societies everywhere, the radical sameness of their inhabitants, and the fact of near limitless human malleability—crossed the line that separates political philosophy from religious faith, or even from a cult whose primary aim is to control its members in thought and action. Liberals believe that liberalism, their idea of the Way, the Truth, and the Life for mankind, has demonstrated to the satisfaction of rational and educated persons that it can govern the world justly and efficiently and that it effectively "controls its destinies," which are converging by a sure dialectical process toward the End of History under liberal tutelage. Regarding ritual, prayer, and spiritual exercises, liberals have been engaging publicly, *en masse,* and *ad nauseam* in these observances ("demonstrations") since 1848, and they have redoubled their efforts since January 20, 2017. As for principles of everyday conduct, they have codified these in an elaborate and absolute system they call "ethics," rigidly enforced. And beyond these things, liberals have a gallery of saints, many of them martyrs, that after a mere two and a half centuries is large enough to fill the cathedral of Chartres and includes such notables as Gandhi, Martin Luther King, and Matthew Shepherd, who, as liberal saints should be, are faithful representations of the morality of modern liberalism: the first a spiritual fraud whose chief accomplishment was to create social and political messes he later walked away from; the second, despite his admirable personal bravery, a plagiarist, serial adulterer, and alleged communist (cf. *Plagiarism and the Cultural Wars: The Writings of Martin Luther King, Jr., and Other Prominent Americans,* by Theodore Pappas); and the third an aggressive adept at buggery and a dealer in drugs. And liberals have miracles, among them cleansing all men of their sins by denying sin and murdering the Deity by incantation—writing pseudo-scholarly treatises, that is, asserting His death. Having re-divinized Western politics by proclaiming the death of God, liberalism, the revolutionary secular commitment that has stepped up to His abandoned place, has arranged for His burial by the New Atheists who, dishonestly and with a fine disdain for rationality, deny the rationality of theism generally and the Christian faith in particular by selective ignorance and deliberate misrepresentation of the classical proofs of the necessary existence of a Creator, while professing a self-assured atheism through the blindest of self-blinding faiths.

Liberalism was not originally a type of religion at all, having coexisted more or less comfortably with Christianity (though not with Islam and voodoo) for some time. But the transformation of science from essentially a metaphysical enterprise into a practical one that values material effectiveness over pure truth, and the subsequent issue of democratic politics from liberal political theory, ensured a rupture between the two things. For liberal theorists and democratic practitioners alike, Christianity seemed too humanly humble, too pessimistic, too confining a creed to fit with liberal and democratic aspirations for individuals and societies, an insult to pride of life and of the mind; increasingly so, as scientific power advanced together with human control over nature to the point where men could imagine becoming like gods themselves, and democratic theorists and politicians encouraged citizens in ever more egalitarian democracies to fancy themselves every man a king. Because the scientific spirit and the democratic one—the ultimate expressions of human pride—decline to subordinate themselves to anyone or anything, liberal political thought was driven, inadvertently at first, to invent a new religion for itself to supplant the Christian one that constrained it, and that it believed humanity had outgrown.

The liberal religion, like Christianity, is an improving religion, but there the likeness ends. Christianity looks inward and outward and upward, liberalism outward and forward. Liberalism encourages its adherents to feel proud, confident, and uncritical about themselves; Christianity counsels humility, self-criticism, penitence—and penance. Liberalism works toward the end of history, Christianity toward the end of time. Christianity is a religion of self-denial and even of mortification, liberalism of self-indulgence and self-gratification, exactly suited to the needs (and wants) of democratic-capitalist-industrial-commercial-consumerist societies. Liberalism substitutes what it calls "ethics," which can be satisfied by lip-service and virtue-signaling, neither of which costs anyone anything, for Christian morality, whose strictures, being divine, are frequently observed only painfully by fallen men and women. Christian morals condemn all too human desires, though they do so in mercy and understanding; liberal ethics blesses them as being natural and human and therefore healthy and liberating, as the modern social and psychological sciences insist they are. And since liberalism has recently found the freedom to act according even to nature insufficient and repressive, liberal theory, impressed and inspired by medical technique, has lately discovered human nature to be actually nonexistent—a mere social construct—allowing people living in liberal societies the freedom not only to have whatever they wish but to *be* whatever they want, regardless of their irrelevant chromosomes.

Hence liberalism, at liberty to deny traditional morality based on man's unique status as a son of God, replaces it with an ethical system that is natural, normative, relative, and directed toward personal "fulfillment," individual happiness and contentment, social peace, political harmony, and—the ultimate goal—uninterrupted economic and technological advancement and the infinite wealth and freedom they supposedly bring. Lastly, liberalism demands no sacrifice from its devotees—no painful personal ones anyhow, since liberal sacrifice is collective and impersonal, and so in a way abstract—or simply someone else's, and almost always that of the One Percent, which, though mostly liberal itself, employs a staff of accountants and lawyers to minimize its generosity. All this explains why liberalism is the convenient faith that asks nothing of its followers save their willingness to deny their own humanity in exchange for enjoying the life of a happy herd of domesticated animals grazing across endlessly green parks shaded by luxuriant trees and carpeted by perennial flowers.

Nevertheless, the liberal religion has a critical weakness that is certain to bring it down in time. It is the final inability of men and women not infected by the liberal virus to believe that their humanity is illusory—but also that human nature is divine, or the closest thing there is in the universe to divinity. This explains men's instinctual urge to worship a higher Being or beings, and in worshipping to make sacrifice to them. It is a fatal mistake to ask too much of people. It is fatal also to ask too little of them. For our human nature, self-subordination and sacrifice are deeply painful, but also deeply satisfying—and *true*. Adoration, which so far as I know is something unique to the Christian religion, is not exactly the same thing as worship, but it is equally rewarding, as the Catholic Church understood in Her institution of the Adoration of the Blessed Sacrament. We humans have a human need to adore, and if the object of fitting and proper adoration—the Holy Sacrament, the Blessed Virgin Mary—is removed from our sight, we will adore Madonna and Taylor Swift. Which is bad enough, but not as bad as adoring Hillary Clinton and Elizabeth Warren, much as liberals want Americans to do.

It is a fact that while one of the other three major world religions (Buddhism), owing to its vague transcendent nature, demands less in the way of sacrifice and general human inconvenience to its believers than Christianity asks of Christians (a Chinese Buddhist once assured me, whether truthfully or not, that I could be a Buddhist as well as a practicing Catholic), the other (Islam) is a religion that from its beginnings has encouraged by its laws and scriptures acts of inhuman cruelty. The liberal religion has nothing in common with the Islamic faith—it is, rather, its exact opposite. Thus liberals' emotional defense of Islam, their siding with it against Christianity though obviously it is everything liberals accuse Christianity of being, is the supreme example of liberalism's fundamental hypocrisy. It is choosing Barrabas over Christ: "Anyone but Him!" The convenient religion is neither God's religion, nor man's, but the breathless, unfeeling, unthinking, unseeing idol designed by a vast international committee operating over three centuries to suit its own purposes. It is yet another proof, as if any were needed, that men will not understand themselves until they are forced to violate their own nature, and thus begin to understand, and—as we are seeing in the international reaction against liberalism today—to insist upon that understanding.

2. The Easiness of Being Liberal

Liberals are keen to sniff out and condemn "privilege," by which they mean the superior education, the affluence, the influence, and the comfort enjoyed by well-connected, well-born white people, usually imagined by them as political conservatives. None of this has anything to do with privilege in the historical sense of the word, which is something else entirely. Before the 20th century, a "privilege" designated a special right, immunity, or benefit granted by sovereigns to persons in reward for having performed a special service, or services, for them. Progressive liberals regularly exhort whites to "check their privilege" with respect to non-whites, never imagining that as liberals they enjoy innumerable privileges of their own that are glaringly obvious to non-liberals.

No one in contemporary Western society is more privileged than the ostentatiously liberal citizen who, so far from hiding his light under a bushel, swings it to and fro like a railway signalman giving the all-clear to the onrushing unstoppable HST, the Dialectical Express. Liberals today are the beneficiaries of privileges non-liberals do not enjoy, among them preference in hiring, attention paid to their enlightened persons, recognition granted to their achievements, respect for their opinions on every subject, and social deference in politically mixed company in those nowadays rare instances when liberals and conservatives come into social proximity with one other. Being liberal today means never having to watch your tongue, or apologize for your opinions. Being illiberal, or anti-liberal, on the other hand, means putting up with accusations of saying or writing "offensive" things, while enduring patiently and in silence daily offenses offered by liberal speakers, liberal writers, liberal colleagues, and liberal neighbors. It means needing to seek out more or less obscure journals, radio and television programs, and newspapers while being hammered by the ubiquitous, unavoidable politically correct mass media. It means doing your best in church to concentrate on prayer while shutting your ears to the liberal sermons and the sacred Musak wafting from the choir loft, and avoiding the liberal activists who dominate the lay work in the parish. If you are a church musician, it means having to accommodate your material, style, and technique to the tastes of liberal philistines who resent and resist high art ("elitist'), expertise in execution and musical interpretation ("pretentious"), and anything "old" and "out of date" ("reactionary"). For many centuries, the churches were the primary educators of their flocks in letters, music, the fine arts, and languages, as well as the Bible and theology, but with the arrival of what Evelyn Waugh called the Century of the Common Man, when exposing the Faithful to anything above the level of crass plebian culture became an affront to the lowest common social and intellectual denominator, they readily abandoned that mission.

As the critic J. O. Tate has observed, vulgarity has replaced majestic purple mountains and fruited plains as our physical environment, and tasteful mess, delicacy, restraint, and balance as our mental and emotional one. Many liberals deplore the commercial and public culture that produced and sustains it as the crude expression of the souls of the American deplorables who support Donald Trump for president. Yet so infused is popular culture by subliminal liberal propaganda inserted there by its largely liberal creators, promoters, and interpretive "artists" that even liberals who hold their noses in the presence of this noisome banality are content to tolerate it on behalf of furthering their political and social ends. It is true that many of these mass purveyors of vulgarity are not really liberals but rather political conservatives in the sense that they vote Republican from their personal financial interest, yet tend also to be people whose spiritual brutishness permits them to swim happily in the continental cesspool that has become the national swimming-hole. These people consort contentedly with liberals for commercial ends, no offense taken from any but their colleagues' more flagrant political heresies (usually those having to do with tax policy).

Western people today, conservatives and liberals alike, experience the prevailing liberal social atmosphere as the unquestioned norm of modern life, whether they know it or not. And even if they do know it, they are terrified of being thought "abnormal" by their fellows by dissenting from it. Moreover, middle-class Americans, since at least around the turn of the 20th century and increasingly during the 1920s and 1950s, have ranked "niceness" and "being nice" among the cardinal moral and civic virtues. In more conservative eras niceness has meant being "respectable." But from the 1980s forward as life in the Western democracies has been progressively liberalized, "nice" has evolved as the equivalent of "liberal," and "liberal" has come to mean "nonjudgmental," "tolerant," "anti-critical," and open to every new thing, every new value, every new standard approved by liberals as something every citizen has a moral duty to approve.

What the British call "virtue signaling" is only one sign among many of this. Virtue signaling is an act of affirmation of some liberal value or shibboleth, intended to establish or reaffirm the sender's reputation as a socialized, politically correct, and tolerant person. Even the strongest political conservatives—people who believe in the free market and resist statism, support a strong military defense, and go to church every Sunday—participate in virtue signaling to display their liberal (small-l) intentions, maintain social harmony, and compensate for their illiberal opinions regarding fundamental political, economic, and social issues. In this way they unconsciously become acclimated to liberal society until they are no more aware of it than they are of the natural atmosphere they breath—even if the liberal social reality breaks in upon them occasionally, like a bad-tasting, bad-smelling, choking smog.

Virtue signaling is one aspect of the urgent exhortative tone characteristic of modern liberal society—the cheer-leading "Okay-guys-let's-all-go-out-today-and-do-our-ethical-thing!" society. The spirit behind exhortative liberalism is purely liberal-bourgeois, yet its pedigree traces from the civic boosterism of the conservative bourgeoisie of the 1920s, to whom Sinclair Lewis's fictional character of the decade gave the name "babbitry." Modern liberals, with different or opposed social and political agenda, look down their noses at the middle-class babbitry persistent in the civic activities of the Chamber of Commerce, Rotary, the Lions Club, and the Elks Club, though those of the League of Women Voters, Emily's List, the Children's Defense Fund, and Planned Parenthood are similarly naïve, smug, and vulgar. In fact there has always been an intimate connection between liberalism and social and intellectual vulgarity, beginning with the *nouveau-riche* men of commerce, industry, and public affairs who pushed for liberal political systems and liberal economic policies early in the 19th century, and including the pseudo-philosophical liberal theorists who laid the foundations for a system characterized by high intellectual vulgarity, mental *naïveté*, and a dangerous misunderstanding of the world, and of man. Liberalism is wholly compatible with the moral, aesthetic, and political vulgarity of modern commercial-democratic society.

The town of 30,000 people where I've lived for 22 years is set high in the Rocky Mountains, geographically speaking, but well below sea-level from the cultural standpoint despite being the seat of a state university. The local newspaper was founded in 1881, the school five years later. I haven't looked into the paper's archives, but I imagine that its character in the days when the town's economy was based on railroading, ranching, and logging differed drastically from what it is today, when the paper ranks easily with *The New York Times* in the fervency and abandonment of its politically correct liberalism. Much of the change obviously reflects the influence of the university, which, with the exception of those departments devoted to practical fields of study like mining, engineering, and agriculture, is the equal in liberal dementia of any comparable institution back East—whence a great many of its faculty have been imported to the Cowboy State. Much, but not all of it. The remainder is simply an expression of the liberal spirit that in recent decades has infected Main Street, small-town, and middling-city America.

The newspaper is the town's Plaza Fountain, its Versailles Gardens Fountain, its Trevi Fountain of self-conscious, moralistic, virtue-spouting, liberal exhortation. What hard news there is at hand to report daily is buried by alerts, announcements, feature stories, and photographs promoting a variety of "awarenesses," "sensitivities," and other liberal totems: Big Brother and Big Sister, Violence Against Women Week, Race For the Cure events, rallies to save the climate and fight "discrimination against the LGBT community," Latina seminars, safe sex crusades, and Special Olympics weekends. In the *Boomerang's* world, every one "cares," "gives back," "supports," and "tolerates" from morn to set of sun, and – no doubt—in his dreams as well. Matthew Shepherd is the patron saint not only of the Episcopal cathedral, but of the town itself. Once or twice a month some retrograde soul has a brief, unenlightened protesting screed published on the Letters page, but the temerarious dissenters willing to speak their minds even in private conversation are few, as the business class has largely adopted the opinions of the university faculty, partly to avoid the risk of boycott, partly from considerations of perceived social status. It's considered "not nice" to mock, let alone object to, false sentimentality, moralistic self-satisfaction, and virtue signaling, assuming even that people are any longer aware of these things, now as natural seeming a part of the municipal atmosphere as the Union Pacific trains high-balling it through the freight yards, the overflowing bars downtown on Saturday nights, and the ubiquitous message T-shirts advertising (in about equal numbers) commercial products, liberal causes, organizations, and sports teams. (Message T-shirts are another ubiquitous message from the Exhortative Society, delivered by bipedal human billboards who imagine their fellow bipeds care a tinker's damn what products they buy, what left-wing causes they support, or what teams they root for.) It may be, too, that the large majority of Americans have learned unconsciously to accept the liberal media simply as a familiar, unremarkable, and even ignorable element of the liberal atmosphere—the more so for people who take all their news from Fox and never look at any paper beyond the local one.

The world is the liberal's oyster but it is a poisoned oyster. A polluted environment damages everyone and everything, including the masses of human bi-valves who live hermetically sealed up in ideological shells. Shell-life is an easy life, especially when it is part of a vast shell-fish community. But shell-fish too have their predators, capable of breaking through shells to the vulnerable creatures within, softened by long protection from hard reality and experience.

CHAPTER SIX | THE FUTURE OF LIBERALISM

Twenty sixteen was the year that American liberals confidently expected to consolidate the quiet political and cultural revolution they had been effecting for decades in the coming national elections. When the Republican Party nominated Donald J. Trump as its presidential candidate, the apparent miracle was almost enough to cause the Democracy to reconsider the possibility of a Supreme Being; especially since, in the case of His Existence, He was obviously not simply a fellow liberal but a Democrat besides. But instead of victory, election year delivered them and their Gramscian agenda (dating from the early 1960s) a setback at the polls as considerable as it was shocking. God seemed suddenly to revert to the status of myth once more; a myth at once childish and sinister, a trick on religiously-minded people who then employed it as a cynical means to rally the credulous opiated masses.

1. The Long Retreat Through the Institutions

The "long march through the institutions" advocated by Antonio Gramsci after the Great War, when the proletariat had vitiated Marx's prophesy that international catastrophe would provoke the working class to rise up as a man against their capitalist-bourgeois exploiters by enthusiastically enlisting in the capitalists' armies to fight on behalf of their native *patriae*, seemed to have been arrested by a contrary force the liberals immediately fingered as "populist." Gramsci had argued that the workers had been corrupted by materialism and a "false consciousness" of their situation, deprived of the revolutionary spirit the Marxist dialectic attributed to them. Obviously, they were not the crowbar revolutionary elites could employ to overturn bourgeois-capitalist society. But where physical violence on the part of mob had failed to materialize, subversive efforts by the revolutionary intelligentsia would succeed as they surreptitiously sapped and weakened all the major Western institutions starting

116

(and ending) with Christianity, which Gramsci and the like-minded fellows of the Frankfurt School correctly perceived as the ultimate Enemy, by discrediting and mocking the intellectual, philosophical, religious, and moral structures that had nourished and supported them for millennia. The program of the Frankfurt School, which moved to the United States in the 1930s when its members were granted entry to America as refugees from National Socialism, was substantially the agenda of advanced liberalism, which took much from it. And advanced liberalism was, roughly speaking, what the winning portion of the American electorate voted to reject when it elected Donald Trump president that fall. Were it not for the fact that the vast majority of these voters had never been liberals (much less revolutionaries) in the first place, one might plausibly describe what happened on 8 November, 2016, as the American Thermidor, as Leon Trotsky described Stalin's accession to power as "the Soviet Thermidor."

The opposition of the moderate Girondins caused Robespierre and his fellow sanguinary radicals of "The Mountain" to resort to their mass execution, the proximate cause of the onset of the Reign of Terror. The liberal reaction to the Trump presidency never even remotely approached that, of course, though the rhetorical ferocity of Trump's opponents does suggest that violence is in the hearts of many of them. Nevertheless it has exposed the illiberality of modern liberal democrats and the societies they have built, and the profoundly reactionary nature of their response to "populist" opposition, especially when the opposition is successful. From the first day of President Trump's administration, liberals and the left as a whole began talking like Burkeans, while conservatives and "populists" have tried to return politics in America to Burkean principles that acknowledge and respect the political competency and innate human wisdom of ordinary citizens. Modern liberals, who until the previous year had praised and encouraged authenticity, spontaneity, creativity, eccentricity, free spiritedness, originality, iconoclasm, irreverence, social and individual relaxation to the point of laxness (and beyond), informality, sexual freedom, liberation from "structure", the abolition of boundaries and of rules, regulations, and protocol, suddenly professed to be shocked by the authenticity, spontaneity, iconoclasm, and irreverence shown by the Trump administration, from the President himself on down through his subordinates and in every department of the governmental, political, and diplomatic process. No American president—probably no modern head of state anywhere—has been so utterly unconventional, so *genuine*, as Donald Trump was (and is), yet his liberal critics persist in remaining stubbornly unimpressed. Indeed, they are overwhelmingly hostile. Nearly everything the former President has said or done, in or out of office, at home or abroad, in public or privately, in his relations with federal employees or foreign leaders, has been met by a chorus of outraged protest from the left. "But that just isn't how it's *done!*"… "He's breaking with America's policies toward our NATO allies for *decades!*" … "Senior diplomats at the State Department are leaving in *droves!*"… "His recognition of Jerusalem as the capital of Israel destroys the arrangement that has kept the peace in the Middle East *for ages!*"…"He wandered over—just like that—and spoke with Putin without anyone *else* present—a breach of diplomatic protocol!" (Putin taught himself English some time ago.) "He's trying to reverse bipartisan policy toward Russia for *years!*"… "But the *whole world* has been moving toward free trade agreements for *decades!*"… "He praised *western civilization* in Hamburg! No American president has *ever* done such a thing!"…. "*Every other country in the world* voted at the UN against recognizing Jerusalem as the capital of Israel!"… "He made fun of Dear Leader Jr. at the *United Nations*! *Another* breach of protocol—he embarrassed the U. S. in front of the *whole world!*"… "He rammed through the first comprehensive overhaul of the U. S. tax code in *30 years!*"… "He's removing decades of regulations from the statute books that have accumulated over *half a century!*"…"Communicating with the public by Tweet is *completely inappropriate* for a president of the United States!"… "Kellyanne Conway sat on the gold sofa in the Oval Office *with her feet up—lèse majesté!*"… "He drinks *Diet Coke and eats fish fillets from MacDonald's!*"… (Big Macs and French fries were presidential and endearing when Bill Clinton was Chief Executive. And if Mr. Trump dined on caviar and champagne every noon he'd be accused of the elitism of the One Percent and running up the deficit in a single breath.) You might think that liberals, who by nature find change, iconoclasm, and informality refreshing, would have applauded admiringly. The fact that they responded with spitballs and raspberries instead shows how profoundly reactionary, in the contextual sense at least, advanced liberalism has become in its desire for a very illiberal political and cultural stasis and strict regimentation in everything. For liberals, custom, habit, prescription, precedent, prejudice and (all revered and extolled by Edmund Burke) have become God terms since liberals appropriated the falsely termed conservative Establishment and made it virtually unassailable by all challengers. The world, for decades until now, has been their oyster bed, and liberals are willing to fight to the death to hold onto it for themselves.

They mean to do this by consolidating their political victories, and the power and success those victories have won for them. Indeed, consolidation seems at this point the logical, necessary, really the sole choice available to them, since it is hard to see how the liberal ideology can advance conceptually and in reality much beyond the welfare state in which almost half the population pay no taxes and unwed mothers are married to the government; the sexual revolution; women's liberation; gay marriage; transgenderism, the abolition of the two sexes, and the invention of several new ones; the erasure of national borders and the melding of national cultures; the globalization of the economy and absolute freedom of immigration and migration; forcible secularization and the persecution of the Christian churches; and the replacement of learning and traditional education by the absurdist propaganda ginned up in the advanced kindergartens that are dignified today by the name of universities. It is hard to see what institutions remain for the left to march through, what priceless treasures within them to smash, as ISIS's fighters did in Palmyra and elsewhere. It can only consolidate or retreat, something it will never do voluntarily, only under irresistible pressure and forcible assault.

In America, the liberal reaction to Trump's presidency was more extreme than the response by British liberals to Brexit and by German ones to the Alternative for Germany's winning 94 seats in the Bundestag in 2017, though it is impossible to say the how the French might have greeted the election of Marine Le Pen as president of the Fifth Republic. This may be down to the fact that advanced liberalism in these post-modern times is far more advanced in America, whose stamp it bears, than in France, where the Revolution at the end of the 18th century established liberalism and the left in their classical and modern forms that lasted for almost 200 years, and in England. (It is true that the left in Europe and in Great Britain always sounded as deranged on the subject of Trump during his presidency as its American counterpart did.) The insane opposition to the President at home probably reflected (beyond the fact that he was the president of the United States) America's greater social complexity produced by her continental extent, geographical differences, and by the racial, ethnic, social, and religious diversity created by two centuries of mass immigration from around the world. On the other hand, the relative intellectual and emotional restraint displayed by the *conservative* European opposition to the *liberal* establishment—the converse of the present American situation—may indicate that the oppositionists feel more confident than partisans of the liberal "Resistance" on the Western side of the Atlantic do, where the two-party system often seems to members of both parties an all-or-nothing affair, for so long at least as the party in power controls the federal government. Under a multiparty system, opposition parties (the Alternative for Germany, for instance) paradoxically feel a degree of security in their minority status, which may persist beyond the next election and into another coalition government.

Also, America's greater racial and cultural diversity and the identity politics that these have fostered mean that the percentage of American citizens who are fundamentally anti-American appears a good deal larger than the percentage of anti-British Britons in the United Kingdom, of anti-French Frenchmen in France, and even of anti-German Germans in Germany. (Consequently, it is fair to wonder whether the United States remains in any real sense a country at all, while Britain, France, and Germany—and the other nations of Europe—are still very much themselves, as their growing nationalist antipathy toward the European Union shows.) Finally, it is an interesting question whether the "populist" anti-liberal movement in Europe has made greater progress against the left and liberalism than its counterpart in the United States has done.

In the past several years much has been written on both sides of the Atlantic about the crisis and even the end of liberalism, and the reasons for its failures. It seems only common sense to suggest that the future of liberalism, its intellectual and political systems, will depend on two things. The first is whether the majority of national publics (mainly in the West, but elsewhere too) will wish to continue to live under the international regime liberal government, liberal ideology, and liberal culture have constructed since 1945—or not. The second is whether, even if they do, advanced liberalism in government is simply too unrealistic in its aims, too self-contradictory in its commitments, too expensive in operation, and too dysfunctional to survive; also whether, as an intellectual system, it can continue to satisfy intellectually the civilized minority who think seriously about serious human things in a supernatural context, including what used quaintly to be called "the Truth."

Among the many signs that the liberal system is self-destructive, and therefore unsustainable, is the mass hysteria that broke out in October 2017 following allegations of sexual harassment against the filmmaker Harvey Weinstein and ballooned instantly into the #MeToo movement, grounded in the notion that all men are priapic monsters and the insistence that anyone who questions the stories women who claim to be victims of priapism tell (often decades after the asserted incident) is himself a monster poised to rape (if male), or (if female) a sexual quisling, probably a kept woman, and certainly a traitor to her sex. It took a few months for resistance to the resistance to take shape among the rational portion of the female population, including many feminists who argue that #MeToo is anti-feminist in its assumption that women are fragile creatures who, in the absence of strong and honorable men at their side, need defending by the government and the courts, the majority of whose members are still male. Since the sexual harassment problem, allegedly endemic in morally free-wheeling post-Christian society, is plainly among the many unanticipated by-blows of the sexual revolution, #MeToo exposes the logically and politically irresolvable confrontation between sexual libertinism for everyone—male, female, and other—and the claims of feminism. Here is but one of a myriad instances of the modern liberal revolution, the sworn champion of everyone but also of his irreconcilable enemy, like every revolution in history devouring its own while its clients, in turn, fall upon and devour each other.

2. Suicidal Liberalism

The refugee crisis seven years ago in Europe, and the response of the various European governments and of the European Commission, surrealistic as it seems, make sense only if one understands that the agony of contemporary Europe (like that of the United States) is the agony of liberalism, whose contradictions have suddenly caught up to it with the speed and force of a tsunami that has taken even liberalism's fiercest critics by surprise. Liberals, we can see now, are prepared to sacrifice not only their respective nations, but the liberal order itself to the enforcement of liberal ideology in its most abstract form. Clearly Angela Merkel is resolved never to forget the crimes of the Third Reich, but more than seven decades after Hitler's fall she would have done far better to recall her personal sufferings as a child and a young woman under the East German regime, an ordeal from which she ought to have learned the nihilistic consequences of attempting to translate ideological theory into political practice.

On Christmas Eve 2015, in Cologne, 1,500 of what witnesses described as dark-skinned youths from the Middle East and North Africa, many if not most of them heavily inebriated in violation of the laws of the Prophet they propose to impose on Christian Europe, surrounded hundreds of young women and robbed and grabbed and groped them, oblivious to the *polizei* standing helplessly by; raped several more, and shut down a central train station. In short order 653 people had lodged complaints with the Cologne police, who were holding four accused criminals in custody. Also in short order, the federal police identified 32 suspects, 22 of them "asylum seekers." It took the department and the German government days to acknowledge the atrocity, while the news media remained silent in a notable departure from the liberal ideal of an informed society. Identical attacks occurred in Hamburg, Stuttgart, Frankfurt, and Nuremburg, and the head of the federal criminal police claimed that the mass assaults were being loosely organized between cities. When the Cologne attack was acknowledged—again, belatedly—the media treated it as a surprising and wholly untoward occurrence, a phenomenon unlikely to occur ever again. In fact, attacks like it had been happening since 2014 in Sweden, where large groups of young men whom the police described as "so-called refugee groups primarily from Afghanistan" sexually harassed girls attending a music festival, one of them aged twelve. Police officers in Stockholm were ordered not to cite the suspected perpetrators' nationality or ethnicity in their reports and the facts of the matter were only later released to the public, a segment of which responded by asserting that all men—white, brown, or painted blue; natives, refugees, or (presumably) terrorists—are alike, and behave that way. One contributor to the country's largest tabloid, pointing to the fact that white men had been guilty of sexual assaults during the Oktoberfest in Munich earlier that year, argued that people who describe the attackers as North African or Middle Eastern must be racists.

A year after the violence in Sweden, the German government and the German media followed the same formula in their handling of the riot in Cologne. President Merkel and the news people stayed silent as long as they possibly could, and her government was said to have ordered the police knowingly to misrepresent the general refugee crisis in order to avoid unwelcome public reaction. A member of the federal police, speaking anonymously, testified that officers at the borders were under orders not to restrain migrants attempting to escape custody, lest "violence" ensue. There was some confusion concerning whether the police were or were not adequately reinforced on New Year's Eve by the Interior Minister at the request of the police chief, and whether the chief erred in not making his request until too late. He was, in any event, subsequently fired in order to "restore the public faith in the police."

The move failed spectacularly since the disaster was being widely blamed on the force, criticized by a female reporter for the *New York Times* as perhaps having "fail[ed] to anticipate the new realities of a Germany that is now host to up to a million asylum [sic] seekers, most from war-torn Muslim countries unfamiliar with its culture" and trying afterward to hide their incompetence. A female analyst and Turkish native, resident for decades in Germany, put the riot down to Germans who regard the refugees as a burden and a danger instead of a gift that will keep on giving. "We need," she explained, "a new common history, a new shared history," especially in "practical" matters, such as policing. To which the *Times* reporter added helpfully, "This was new terrain for all, and just one taste of the challenges facing Germany and its leader,

Chancellor Angela Merkel, to assimilate a huge new population in an atmosphere of dwindling tolerance and volatile politics." Neither lady thought to mention a part of Arab history and culture presumably worthy of being shared by the West: the *Taharrush gamea,* an Arab sex game whose description corresponds exactly with the assaults in Europe: collective physical harassment and abuse by gangs of young males who take advantage of crowds to insult, proposition, grope, rob, and rape young women, a practice become widespread in the Near East since the political uprisings and demonstrations that accompanied the misnamed Arab Spring and is currently being imported to Europe by the same "asylum seekers," 90 percent of whom are single young men at least as interested in the huge harem they obviously imagine Europe to be as they are in their bodily safety. For liberals, these young savages offer no serious danger. Explain to them today what the romantic mores and customs of Europeans are and they'll be more than happy to conform to them tomorrow! (Wikipedia posted a notice on its site directly above the entry for *Taharrush gamea*: **"This article is being considered for deletion in accordance with Wikipedia's deletion policy."**)

The response in Europe and the United States to these eruptions of barbaric lawlessness and aggression proves just how many of liberalism's historical commitments liberals are prepared to jettison in a crisis such as this one, which directly threatens advanced liberalism's project of "inclusiveness," including the creation of multicultural societies and the eventual dissolution of anything properly describable as the Western nation state.

For instance, liberals have been trying for decades to realize the "risk-free society" in which 100 percent of the population is safe, 100 percent of the time, from unhealthy food, unsafe automobiles and intoxicated drivers, environmental pollution, unhealthy workplaces, dangerous gadgets, dangerous children's toys—and guns. Their vision of a risk-free society is a principal motivation in their campaign in America to have the 2nd Amendment repealed. (Liberals' antipathy toward a heavily armed population capable of defending itself against foreign invaders and, especially, tyrannical liberal government is another.) But gun owners here and on the Continent (and elsewhere, so far as I know) do not celebrate public holidays by ganging up in the streets and robbing and assaulting women, or anyone else. Still, liberal opinion holds that while legal gun owners, as potential though statistically negligible threats to the public safety, should be disarmed by force if necessary, marauding invaders from barbarian cultures are not only tolerable but desirable by peaceable societies in unlimited numbers. Another *Times* reporter, not previously quoted, pleaded (in a "news" article) on the invaders' behalf that, "While the police say the assaults in Cologne were carried out by hundreds of men, even that is a narrow sliver of the more than one million asylum seekers who entered Europe last year." A narrow sliver indeed—but a far, far broader one than the miniscule percentage of gun owners who commit murder, mass murder, and rape with their weapons. Yet liberals propose to render all gun owners defenseless by outlawing and confiscating their firearms weapons under a policy of "zero tolerance" for gun violence.

In another instance, Henriette Reker, the feminist mayor of Cologne, suggested when news of the attacks in her city was finally made public that, "It is always possible [for a woman] to keep a certain distance that is longer than an arm's length from a Muslim rapist." Put differently, a woman's right to the inviolability of her person and her dignity as a woman must be sacrificed when necessary (in this feminist politician's opinion) to a Muslim invader's "right" to both of them. It seemed the Western feminist movement was preparing to surrender its cause to the patriarchal male-chauvinist Moor before a single shot had been fired in the most recent battle for Europe, the clash of civilizations. Liberalism may prove even weaker than Western Christendom in confronting an enemy before whom even oppressed and aggrieved feminists find themselves morally disarmed.

The response of European liberals and of the liberal elites that dominate the various Continental governments and the European Union that tries, with increasingly less success, to dominate and finally to anneal them into a single authoritarian bureaucratic entity ruled by socialist economics and political correctness makes two things abundantly plain. The first is that liberalism has committed itself since the 1950s to the cause of so many distinct, and often naturally opposed, groups and categories of people they consider "victims" that they are intellectually disabled and politically confounded when the interests of one victimized group conflict with those of another: in the present case, women *v.* minorities, immigrants *v.* women. The same goes for the principles liberalism espouses collectively, though they are inherently contradictory: in this case, equality under the law *v.* the need for special treatment for some people; the will of the majority *v.* the moral authority of the minority; public order *v.* disruptive cultural self-expression, and so on. In these vexed situations and similar ones, liberals try to surmount ideological contradiction and intellectual bankruptcy by judging on a purely *ad hoc* basis in the interests of the victim *du jour*, frequently at the expense of the victim of the day before yesterday. This mental operation involves resorting to a good deal of pretentious, vapid, and abstract language—the language of bureaucrats and politicians—that Orwell attributed to moral insincerity and intellectual dishonesty.

Mostly, though, the instinctive and panicked response of liberals on both sides of the Atlantic to the European refugee crisis revealed the degree to which the elites are "alienated" from ordinary people. The word "alienation" is an invention of the Western Left in the 1950s to describe the withdrawal of sensitive and morally superior souls (nearly always liberals or communists) from the materialistic wasteland created by the decadent bourgeoisie. By contrast, the contemporary left uses the word to identify those coarse- spirited and morally obtuse, even wicked, people who cannot tolerate life in enlightened liberal society: "populists," "xenophobes," "nativists," "conservatives," and otherwise unredeemed, and probably unredeemable, folk. For liberals, such people are eminently replaceable and they don't much care who replaces them so long as they hail from multicultural backgrounds and are not white skinned—including the "sliver" who practice *Taharrush gamea* for whom excuses can always be found on behalf of so noble a cause as enfolding the Third World into the Continent. Women and girls of Europe, you have nothing to lose but your chastity!

Liberals have fooled so many people for so much of the time over the past century that they have grown over-confident, despite their ever present fear of the dumb and brutal majority, in the ability of their own propaganda to overwhelm popular opinion and even, through its incantatory powers, to alter reality itself. That confidence, and liberalism's ideological understanding of human nature, are its greatest weakness in this critical moment in Western history, blinding them not only to what is really going on in the world but also to how real people see and understand the contemporary situation. In the liberal imagination, the demonstrable results of mass migration and the Islamization of Europe, since they are insignificant or actually beneficial, are a nasty ploy and an excuse on the part of "right-wing extremists," "xenophobes," and "racists" to oust moderate liberal governments across Europe and crush liberalism itself on the Continent out of simple meanness. This is why the media speak sarcastically of "so-called patriots" and native militias patrolling the streets "in the name of protecting women." It is why the United Nations condemned a bill proposed by the Danish government to confiscate money and valuables from asylum seekers entering the country in order to pay for the costs they incur, on the ground that it would offend their dignity and "could fuel fear, xenophobia and similar restrictions that would reduce—rather than expand—the asylum space globally and put refugees in need at life-threatening risks"; and why others have likened the proposed policy to the seizure of valuables by the Nazis from Jews during the Holocaust. So dangerous a misreading of prevailing public sentiment by European rulers possibly has not occurred since 1848, when revolution convulsed the Continent and brought down governments across it. Should European governments in the 21st century remain deaf and blind to the meaning of the events unfolding under their noses, the Spirit of 1848 may well awaken, and sooner rather than later. This time around it will be rebellion, not revolution, that they have to face.

3. Crescent Moon Over Europe

These events, so deliberately and irresponsibly misunderstood by the left, were imaginatively anticipated with an eerie prescience by Jean Raspail, the late French novelist and explorer who before his death must have experienced a sense of living within the pages of *Le Camp des saints*, his most famous work, as he watched the migrant crisis build in Europe. Immediately upon its publication in 1973, *The Camp of the Saints* was attacked and condemned by the *bien-pensants* of France and Europe, and following its translation into English, by the immediate predecessors of political correctness in the Anglosphere who found the novel racist and otherwise objectionable while refusing to consider whether the events in the story were plausible or not. In fact, Raspail foresaw the future of Europe (and the United States) much more accurately than Orwell had done in *1984*, and even than Huxley in *Brave New World. The Camp of the Saints* was for decades a classic of the underground right, first published in America by Scribner's and since reprinted in cheap editions with small print runs by far less august publishers. That the novel remains underground, in spite of disapproving references made now and again to the historically racist nature of Western society ("It's because of people who think like that that we're in the crisis of xenophobia we're experiencing today!"), speaks volumes about the suicidal nature of the liberal and post-liberal West.

Five decades after Jean Raspail's visionary novel, the tens of thousands of Third World migrants are arriving not just on the coast of southern France but all across Europe. And they are coming on foot, by rubber dinghy, and by train from the Middle East, Africa, and Afghanistan; not aboard a huge flotilla of rusting tramp steamers out of Calcutta. Otherwise, Raspail's fictional scenario of more than four decades ago was realized in 2015 as bands and swarms of migrants push north from Greece and Macedonia toward Hungary, Serbia, Croatia, and Austria, guided by mobile phones and GPS, cheered on by Western politicians, the media, the churches, and crowds of welcoming citizens (Lenin would have recognized the latest generation of useful idiots when he saw them) in a state almost of euphoria, as if the crisis had somehow given new meaning and purpose to the lives of these *blasés* post-modern Western bourgeois and restored their will to live. As in the novel, the liberal facilitators of this migratory tide are all sympathy and no logic. It's no easy thing to turn a catastrophe of Continental scope into soap opera, but the left is hard at the job, as the moralistic hysteria surrounding "the drowned toddler" on the Grecian beach showed. Thousands of "toddlers" perish every minute around the world, but for liberal sentimentalists seeing news photographs amounts to responsibility; to them it seems entirely reasonable that the fate of what remains of the greatest civilization in the history of the world should hinge on a single pathetic event. In a truly remarkable example of cognitive dissonance, *L'Osservatore Romano*, the Vatican's daily newspaper, for 10 September 2015, printed an article praising Jean-Claude Junker, President of the European Commission, for having proposed that member countries be compelled to share 120,000 "refugees" among them (added to the 40,000 previously arrived), hard by another story deploring the persecution by Muslims of Christians in the Middle East and noting that of the 1.5 million Christian coreligionists living in Iraq before 2003, barely 300,000 remain. One wonders whether, had the Turkish army before the gates of Vienna had a few tens of thousands of poor Turkish camp followers at its back, Pope Innocent XI would have begged King Jan Sobieski to relent and surrendered the keys to the city to the Turkish general.

If Locke were right in arguing that liberty requires understanding, after two centuries of democratic revolution European liberals are still not free men and women. Few of them, at any rate, grasp the meaning as well as the magnitude of the threat to their Continent and its civilization. Liberals see at stake what Junker calls "European values," while in reality they are the "universal values" of modern liberalism, not just distinct from but contrary to the Christian moral code that has guided Europe for nearly two millennia. In the current migratory crisis, Western universalism recognizes only individuals and "humanity," with nothing— Europeans, Hungarians, Slovaks, Italians, Frenchmen, and Britons—in between. Still it should be obvious to liberal observers that, beyond the "values" they cherish, nothing less than the physical security of the Continent, its component parts, and their future as historical entities is being endangered by the highly illiberal Muslim invaders from the Near East and North Africa. "Armed, aggressive people cannot enter [Hungary]" an aide to President Orbán told reporters, but the Hungarians seem to be almost the only people capable of understanding the existential threat confronting them.

European defenders of the "refugees," eager to resettle people they consider "guilty" only of exercising their "right to travel," regularly invoke their allegedly "peaceable" nature. (I have a right to travel from my house *into* your house if only I do so "peaceably"—*i.e.*, by kicking the door several times and demanding to be let in, while refraining from putting a revolver to your head.) But the tactics of non-violence have always been morally ambiguous, if not actually dishonest—even a type of scam. Obviously, the illegally disruptive disposition of human bodies is itself violence of a sort—static violence, one might say. Certainly it cannot be justified as an act of reasoning dissent or of rational political debate. And its coercive effort to disarm its antagonists morally and shame them into standing down without having employed the use of force rightfully available to them makes it a fundamentally dishonest tactic. However that may be, the invaders from the Levant perpetrated numerous acts of violence against the Hungarian police, some of whom were targets of concrete chunks hurled at them from the crowds they were under orders to restrain. Though the migrants advanced for the most part quietly, their dogged determination had a definite aggressive edge, a hint that they would not be denied the objective of their trek. But the invasion of a foreign country to claim the benefits its government gives citizens who have contributed their labor and a portion of their income to make those benefits available is demonstrably an act of attempted theft. Germany, the first example of a sovereign country declaring itself a magnet state for the world, is also the first self-sacrificial victim known to history, having welcomed hostile barbarians with open arms, showered gifts and loud hosannas upon them. For Angela Merkel, Jean-Claude Junker, and Western officialdom as a whole, self-defense is not a among the "universal values" to recognize and honor.

Though the fact was easy to miss in the early stages of the migration, the migrants today, unlike Raspail's fictional half-naked Untouchables, are largely representative of their homelands' middle and upper-middle classes, able to pay the smugglers, the boatmen, and the train conductors who help them along the new Aboveground Railroad to the Promised Land; they are among the beneficiaries of the rising standard of living in parts of the Third World. It is untrue in the case of most of them to say, as Raspail did of his Calcuttans, that to refuse them admittance to Europe would be to destroy them. (The alternative, as he saw it, was to destroy ourselves.) Through television, the social media, and the Internet they have been exposed to Western affluence and the munificence of the Western welfare states, learned of the West's commitment to universalism, and grasped its reluctance to act in its own defense. They understand that Western governments consider them simply (and simplistically) as human beings endowed with inalienable rights and worthy of potential entitlements, and they are determined to assert those rights in the court of Western opinion when they go before it. Migrants arriving at the gates of Europe tell officials and reporters, "I want to go to Germany and become an engineer"; or "I want to go to Britain because I have a cousin there and they have good benefits"; or "I don't want to go to Austria because Germany will give me more," with the casual self-assurance of a German citizen in Berlin telling a ticket agent, "It's too cold and damp in Hamburg, I want to go to Munich instead." Beggars *can* be choosers after all, it seems. "Why are they treating us like this?" one "refugee" demanded, referring to his temporary consignment to a Hungarian holding camp. "We expected them to let us in and they attacked us. Why?" a former food inspector from Damascus asked. Previous supplicants seeking admission to Europe lacked entirely the new importunates' arrogantly naïve assumption that they have a right to a warm welcome instead of being met with the native resentment and hostility that are humanly justifiable in the circumstances. "Freedom! Freedom!" they shout, imagining they have a claim on the West to anything they might choose to ask of it. This moral self-assurance, this confidence in the demands they make upon the beneficence of strangers, by itself vitiates those claims. These people are not refugees; they are highwaymen. ("Your money or your civic peace!") "Europe Your Humanity Is Lost!" read one sign held toward the police at the Hungarian border. In all this, the "migrants" themselves are unaware that they are the bearers of a failed, fanatical, brutal, and chaotic civilization whose fatal virus prudent foreigners naturally suspect them of harboring. Montesquieu's nobly exquisite Persia, which was of course a figment of his imagination, has long since been buried under the rubble of its ancient monuments and the sands of time and of the desert.

Liberal opinion, which takes for granted the fundamental responsibility of the West for the crisis, citing its political and military interventions in the Middle East and North Africa, has been echoed ironically by Vladimir Putin and paradoxically by Recep Tayyip Erdoğan, president of a dubious NATO "ally." Perversely, liberals also hold the West—America in particular—guilty for *not* intervening in the Syrian rebellion to oust the legally sitting Syrian president and force hostilities in the region to an end. Lastly, they blame the European Union for failing to institute a comprehensive and coordinated immigration policy across the

26 signatories to the Schengen Agreement, and thus for the drowning of several thousand people in the Mediterranean Sea that encouraged subsequent migrants to choose as an alternative the land route into Europe from the Southeast. After Italy's "populist" government closed the country's ports to rescue ships operated by various charitable NGOs the overland migrations to Southeastern Europe abated greatly, thus encouraging a fresh migratory assault on Spain, incidents of drowning in the Mediterranean increased again. But three years after the great invasion of 2015, the subsequent rise of "populist" anger and organized resistance left Brussels and the members of the EU virtually paralyzed, unable to respond to the liberals' outrage.

The primary historical, like the proximate, cause of the migration out of the Middle East, Afghanistan, Pakistan, and Africa, is not the West's interference there but the nasty and dysfunctional character of the civilizations the migrants are abandoning. Western liberals concur in this explanation so far as they can use it to make a case for granting them refuge in the West; arguing that simply by coming here they have shown themselves to be Westerners at heart, people who yearn to join the modern Western project of universal freedom and enlightenment. They angrily reject, however, the proposition that the "refugees" carry with them the morals and mores of their native cultures. Edmund Burke was one of the wisest men who ever lived, but there is reason to reconsider the wisdom of his opinion that "one cannot indict a people," especially when that people has already indicted itself by desperate attempts at self-escape. The role played by the United States and her allies since 1990 is obviously responsible for much recent Levantine chaos and wickedness. Even so, the history of the region over millennia shows that Western colonialism in the last couple of centuries alone cannot account for its chaotic past. In the historical context, one finds nothing to suggest that America's direct intervention in Syria would have brought a peaceful resolution to the multilateral violence occurring there and in neighboring states, and every reason to suppose that the result would have been the opposite. And it is not Europe that is responsible for the deaths in the Mediterranean, but the corrupt African nations and the human smugglers abetted by the NGOs and ultimately the migrants themselves who chose to risk their families' lives on an irresponsible gamble, trusting to

European rescuers to save them—and lost. Jean-Claude Junker is not Neptune, just an impotent EU functionary.

Few people imagined that Germany, whose eventual re-emergence as the dominant power in Europe was inevitable, would unequivocally assert herself in such circumstances as these. With her country's 20th century past and more immediately her own reputation as the dominatrix of Greece in mind, Chancellor Merkel assumed the role of the migrants' champion and protector in the name of "universal values." In truth, these "values" look suspiciously like German values traceable as much to Germany's bad conscience (which ought to have made peace with itself by now) to modern liberal orthodoxy. Since 2015 we have learned that by no means all of Europe subscribes to the liberal orthodoxy, Eastern Europe especially and in particular Hungary, whose president has justified his refusal to settle Muslim migrants in his country by invoking Europe's "Christian roots." Possibly their Communist history inoculated the East European nations against the anti-Christian bias and multicultural mania Western Europe found irresistible. In any event, Mrs. Merkel's assumption that "universal values" can be prudently applied in social and political dealings with foreigners who are already inseparably attached to highly specific cultural and religious ones is imprudent in the extreme. It could have been fatal to the country she was elected to protect, had not the "populists" and "neo-Nazis" in Germany recognized the danger and resisted her.

Clio has her good uses, and then again she has her bad ones. In the current crisis, liberals throughout the West have been abusing her shamelessly by invoking painful emotional memories and images from the last intra-Continental war to discredit every form of resistance to a subtly aggressive invasion by people from beyond the boundaries of Europe, as reporters have juxtaposed the processing centers of Hungary and Austria, the bodily numbering of detainees with felt-tip pens, the packed railway carriages on their way to the centers, and the shouting gesticulating passengers leaning from the train windows with the cattle cars, concentration camps, and gas ovens of the 1940s. The implied comparisons are immoral, as well as cheap. Jobbik in Hungary, PEGID in Germany, the Northern League and the Five Star Movement in Italy, and the National Front in France were not demanding that the migrants be set to hard labor, let alone gassed, only that they be refused sanctuary in Europe. Leo Strauss, the political philosopher and a political liberal, rejected the proposition that foreigners unhappy in their own countries have a natural right to emigrate to societies more successful, pleasant, and humane than their own; they have, after all—as Aristotle argued—the alternative of establishing a comparable regime for themselves at home. One civilization can neither remake another nor rescue it without destroying itself in the attempt. The Middle Eastern refugees (never mind the Afghan, Asian, and African ones), having no valid moral claim on the West, should look to their own people for help and support, beginning with the extremely wealthy Saudis.

The future of Europe will be determined by her willingness to recognize the Muslim invasion for what it is and respond proportionately to the threat. So far, only the Eastern bloc of the EU, and more recently Italy, have demonstrated the necessary firmness to act. "It is absolutely unacceptable to have Greece emptying its refugee camps and sending people towards Croatia via Macedonia and Serbia," a Croatian interior minister complained. "The real solution would be the EU regaining control over its own borders," Hungary's foreign minister said. "The quota system is unenforceable. The conditions for its implementation are not there." Prime Minister Orbàn has been more direct than anyone in refusing to apologize for his uncompromising policies. Millions of migrants, he said, are "laying siege" to Europe and threatening the Continent. "The migrants are not just banging on our door," he added, "they are breaking it down," and he backed up his words by preparing to send the army to the Hungarian border. The spirit of anti-liberal resistance shown by Orbàn spread to the rest of Europe—Great Britain (Brexit), France (where even President Macron enforced French immigration law and has been emphasizing principles and *laicité*), Austria (Sebastian Kurz, the young chancellor who stepped down from office recently), Poland, Slovakia, Italy, and even the Netherlands—and with it demands by the governments of EU members that the Schengen Agreement guaranteeing freedom of movement across the European Union be suspended or repealed, and that Brussels establish a secure external border. The recent crisis on the border between Poland and Belarus, which threatened Warsaw directly and the other 26 members of the European Union indirectly with 200,000 migrants from the Middle East and Central Asia (employed against them by Minsk and the Kremlin in a campaign of what is being called hybrid warfare), is greatly aggravating tensions within the bloc as the Poles demand that Brussels pay the cost of the Polish-Beylarusian boundary.

The West has been worshipping at the shrine of liberal democracy for more than two centuries. Now that liberalism has turned illiberal, the time has come to drag the lady from her grotto by the hair and discover whether, in a time of supreme crisis, "the old bitch gone in the teeth" (Ezra Pound's phrase) can make good on the promises that have been made on her behalf. Or not.

4. One Nation Divided

The great liberal dream of a united Europe—more precisely, a thoroughly melded and homogenized Europe without national boundaries or national cultures and committed to universalist principles, a universalist ethical system, and a single "European" culture shaped by liberal "values" disguised as traditional European ones—is dying. This leaves the Continent to relapse in time into a neighborhood of discreet nations, each one characterized by its historical culture and political structure and demarcated by national borders. This is part of what may be called the decline to normal. It is happening in the Old World. And it is happening in the United States, as a too-complex and badly integrated (though overly centralized) empire goes the way of such previous historical assemblages. With the collapse of the European Union and the weakening of social and political bonds within the U.S.—the first fruit of the liberal project—liberalism as an international force will vanish with them.

Since 1892 when the original text was composed, the Pledge of Allegiance has been revised three times. Viewed chronologically, the alterations appear to have aimed at a greater specificity, but also at a wider and deeper self-assurance. The current text, dating from 1954, capitalizes "Nation" and adds "under God," as if the authors (a committee, no doubt) suspected that American citizens needed to have their sense of nationhood and security under the special protection of the Deity reinforced for them. Today, when 1954 seems as distant as 1054, it is tempting to

discern in the history of this brief document an anxiety, perhaps unconscious, regarding America's future that was not only justified, but
prescient and almost prophetic. At the end of the second decade of the
21st century, the political and moral dissolution of the United States is
as obvious as her fundamentally changed political form; no longer a republic, nor "one Nation under God, indivisible," nor a country "with liberty and justice for all," but a decaying empire with one law for its
governors and their allies and another for its subjects, one form of logic
for the governing class and its specially protected clients and another,
parallel one for the common majority. From the vantage of the present
moment, the United States, far from being the "exceptional nation," appears quite an ordinary one—perhaps not even a nation at all, owing to
her preternaturally accelerated history of less than two centuries and a
half, made possible by her freedom from geographical constraints before
1890 and foreign ones up to 1914, and the unprecedented pace modernity has kept since her founding in 1789. Two and a quarter centuries,
viewed in historical context, are, historically speaking, a very short space
of time for a nation to take form in. So perhaps America is truly exceptional for being a not-nation that has got away with the pretence and
appearance of being a real one for as long as she has done.

America is an historical anomaly chiefly for reasons of time and
space. The United States began as a newly joined assembly of English
colonies, dissimilar in many ways, stretching along the North American
coast; a seaboard republic that only 14 years later became a continental
empire when President Jefferson in 1803 arranged the Louisiana Purchase that added 828,000,000 square miles to the young nation's territorial extent, more than doubling her original size and adding an
indigenous population of perhaps a few million people whose presence
changed her demographic and social complexion radically and forever.
Westward expansion led to the annexation of Texas and the Mexican-
American War that added Mexico's northern and northwestern territories to the Union, and with them a substantial Spanish and Indian
population. Less directly, it was responsible for the War Between the
States a dozen years later that freed the black slave population, natural-
ized it, and enfranchised it. Indirectly too, by force of expansionist habit,
it encouraged imperial expansion into the Caribbean Sea and the Pacific

Ocean that brought on the Spanish-American War and the acquisition of the Philippines, Hawaii, and other Pacific islands and with them their own remote peoples and cultures. Concurrently with these vast territorial and human gains, a steady stream of immigrants, mainly from the British Isles and notably from Catholic Ireland, began in the 1820s. Well before the Civil War the stream had widened to include German immigrants and others from northern Europe. After the war and the reunion of the states, the stream became a wave whose origins now included southern and eastern Europe. The new immigration, though prompted by political revolutions in Europe, was encouraged and facilitated—actually demanded—by American industrialists seeking cheap labor to build the vast industrial plant they were creating continentally. Rapid industrialization thus joined territorial expansion, immigration, and imperialism as a major transformer of the original nation, not yet a century old.

A major result of this transformation was a growing loss of national identity, as real as it was deeply felt and sharply perceived, and popular uncertainty concerning the reality of democracy in America and her prospects and plans for the future that aided the imperial program of extending democracy to the little brown brothers overseas. This benefitted President Wilson's efforts to take the United States into a European conflict he represented to the country as a war to make the world safe for democracy—America's first ideological war. Her participation in the Great War, despite the two more or less isolationist decades that followed the peace treaty that ended it, guaranteed the country's eventual total commitment to Europe, first in World War II and then during the Cold War: a second ideological Armageddon that completed America's metamorphosis from a republic to a world empire. It was for ideological reasons too (liberalism at home, Cold War propaganda abroad) that Congress passed the Immigration and Nationality Act of 1965 that opened up America to immigration from the non-European nations and transformed the country—demographically, culturally, politically, and economically—in the space of a few decades. So rapid, so many, and such foundational changes wrought upon a wide-flung and loosely knit society over a mere 23 decades are not conducive to nation building, a process that in the case of all pre-modern countries—Great Britain, France, Germany, Italy, and the great non-Western ones including China and

India—took centuries and even millennia to accomplish. So it is reasonable to argue that America is not, and never has been, a nation in the true sense of the word, and that she is unlikely to retain even the semblance of one in future. The signs are all around us.

Since 1965, far-sighted critics with an understanding of history and human nature have warned that the new immigration will lead, and is leading, to the balkanization of the United States of America. Democrats and liberals, as well as radicals, have steadfastly denied the likelihood, or even the possibility, of such a thing; whoever argues otherwise, they say, is a racist and a xenophobe. All human beings, the left insists, are precisely alike except in the most superficial ways; their cultures too are minor variations on one another and so are their religions, including such radically opposed ones as Christianity and Islam, Judaism and Buddhism, Confucianism and Santería. Liberals persist in maintaining this fantasy, whose falsity is demonstrated by liberalism itself in its new guise of identity politics, whose rise coincides exactly with the arrival of scores of millions of non-white, non-Christian, and non-Western peoples, and whose program is ideally fitted to the phenomenon, as well as a reflection of it. (It is possible that liberalism's latest obsession with sexual identity is a clever means, whether conscious or not, to disguise the underlying racial one.)

"Balkanization" is no longer a possibility, near or remote, for the United States; it is a reality. It is happening right now and it appears unstoppable, for the excellent reason that there has been nothing to stop it since the Biden administration came to power last year to advance the process. Moreover, racial, cultural, and religious balkanization is a major factor responsible for the intellectual and ideological balkanization of the American public, among whose bitter and poisonous fruits is the hatred one half of the country feels for the other half, each living in its separated mental, metaphysical, and emotional world. Both sides, left and right, recognize that the Enemy is not going way, since total victory by the one over the other is impossible in the foreseeable future. In 1861 the United States was a house divided (though not nearly so widely as it is thought to have been). In 2018, she is a house shattered and tottering. You can make two good houses from the separated halves of one house, if that house is big enough and solid enough to start with, but nothing from the violently scattered and half-destroyed fragments of an exploded one—nothing, anyway, that resembles a proper house. America today is comparable to the Roman Catholic Church after 1517, when the initial separation by the Lutherans from Rome led inevitably, in fact and in logic, to a chain of subsequent fissions among the Protestant churches, whose end is not in sight even now. Similarly California, whose immigration, environmental, and other policies are effectively those of a seceded state, is being defied by some of its own towns and counties (Oroville has recently declared itself a "red" sanctuary state) and the city of San Diego which, out of patience with the plague of illegal immigrants, decided several years ago to comply with federal immigration law instead of what passes for it in Sacramento. Fission, once begun, easily becomes uncontrollable; a process that gave humanity the cancer cell and the atom bomb.

Still, more significant than red America's disillusionment with an integral United States is a similar, but opposite, disillusionment on the part of blue America, which has recently begun talking about seceding from the greater continental Republic. Colorado, for instance, which interstate migration over the past couple of decades has changed from a socially and politically conservative state to a progressively blue one, is beginning to think of itself as a progressive regional entity comprised of itself, California, Oregon, and Washington and having little or nothing in common—economically, socially, or politically—with the conservative states north, south, and east of it. Equally interesting and ironic about this development is the fact that this liberal separatist inclination is not a result of immigration from Mexico and Central America and a related irredentist movement, but rather of impatience and disgust on the part of the liberal demographic group that promoted the nationalist cause for two and a half centuries and fought a war between the states in order to preserve an undivided nation in the interest of national ambitions and the nationalist "dream." On this evidence, it appears that the new liberal America has given up on the old liberal America, just as the old conservative one has. It is hard to conceive of a more discouraging word, for the future of the United States of America.

From about the time of the Spanish-American War down to the post-Soviet era, America—*Americans*—were fairly in solidarity with their countrymen against a dangerous and uncertain world, and any perceived threat to their democracy. But since the demise of the Great Satan from the Russian Steppes, that solidarity has been shaken by popular disillusion created by lost or stalemated foreign wars and the expenditure of American blood and fortune on the battlefields of countries Over There, countries many of whose own people, after proving themselves to be unenthusiastic and ineffective allies of the United States, were rewarded by being granted by America's liberal establishment refugee status Over Here. As for democracy, only the politicians profess to believe that the U.S. is any such thing anymore. The majority of Americans are weary of war, weary of financial and human sacrifice, weary of unsavory allies, weary of unpleasantly foreign, unsuitable, and unassimilable hordes arriving from uncivilized places to transform their country into a congeries of vast and crowded International Houses subsidized at their expense. Victor Bulmer-Thomas, an English historian who has spent much time, and taught, in the United States argues in a recent book (*Empire in Retreat: The Past, Present, and Future of the United States*) that the future of the United States is as a post-imperial country; Americans, he says, no longer wish to pay the price of empire. (A future Bulmer-Thomas approves, so long as the transition from empire to republic again is managed responsibly and well.)

The larger and more essential question, which he does not address, is whether it is possible to recreate a new American republic from a people that has ceased to act and even think as a people—a nation. The return to something like the Articles of Confederation might be an answer, or a geographically contiguous collection of political and cultural entities similar to the original 13 colonies, created this time around by the process of voluntary self-segregation by political belief and cultural affinity that has been going on for some time now and seems likely to accelerate. But the future is unreadable, it cannot be planned for; just as America's history from 1789 to the present day was unplanned.

Viewed from the East Coast of North America, the Atlantic Ocean seems to recede eastward toward the country's historical and cultural origins, the relatively gentle surf (save along the rocky coast of Maine) drawing us backward in time and vision. On the West Coast the violent surf, driving in from the ungraspable immensity of the Pacific and crashing against an endless coast of sharp and jagged rock in great bursts and blowing clouds of spray, seems like a huge invisible hand pushing back against the continent, as if to warn, "So far, and no farther." Perhaps, in its premature old age, the nation that never was a nation can look backward upon itself to discover a previously unimaginable future.

* * *

The liberal media, which profess to be distressed by the "divisiveness" of conservative politics, are never more themselves than when sniffing out and deploring violence, and micro-violence, in America—gun violence, police violence, violence against women, violence against children, violence against racial and ethnic minorities, violence against immigrants, violence against Muslims, violence against homosexuals and "transgendered people," violence against foreign countries and cultures, violence against nature—while remaining blissfully unconscious of the verbal violence they commit every moment of the day in print and in pixels in their various publications that, as much as anything, widens the existing divisions among the American public.

The trend began about two decades ago when reporters, columnists, and editorialists discovered and fell helplessly in love with the verb "to bash," which apparently appealed to them as *le mot juste*, having exactly the connotations of graphic physical brutality, emotional viciousness, and deranged hatred they read into the mildest expression of disapproval or criticism of "gays," the "gay life-style," and the "gay community." Almost overnight, "gay bashing" appeared across the media like mushrooms after a spring storm, suggesting wide-eyed devils with teeth like rows of knives smashing in the heads of "gays" with shovels and pickaxes as if they were melons. Suddenly, the most sensitively phrased hint that homosexuality might be something else than a holy calling and homosexuals its adepts, priests, and prophets provoked the instant charge of "gay bashing." Whether or not this sanguinary image caught readers' imagination by appealing to their poetic sense, it certainly captured the fancy of the thousands upon thousands of journalists who discovered they couldn't do without it. "When you find a good thing, *run it into the ground*" was the motto of William Rusher, the late conservative strategist and former publisher of *National Review*. Unlike so much advice, Rusher's Rule is pleasurable as well as easy to follow. So in no time at all the journalistic left was identifying almost anybody who publicly disagreed with, or disapproved of, any member of any social category whose official victim status it recognized as a "basher" of one type or another.

Journalists as a class are—as they have always been—lazy, poorly educated, and highly imitative people of mediocre intelligence and small imagination, as Mencken argued a century ago in a famous essay that President Franklin Roosevelt once cleverly used against him at a Gridiron dinner. When one of them latches onto some neologism, he enters it at once in his tactics and strategy manual and leaves it there until the journalistic fraternity grows bored with it—usually long after the salt has lost its flavor for the public. Meanwhile, they and their colleagues can satisfy their impulse to creativity by widening its field of application—running it into the ground, in short. Thus in the journalistic idiom of today, no politician, journalist, or public figure of any sort "criticizes" another. Instead he, she, it, or zit "lashes out," "slams," "blasts," "skewers" (or "bashes") the person on the receiving end of the criticism, disagreement, or correction, a choice of words intended somehow to moralize and goose what might otherwise be a dullish story, or even no story at all, by summoning to the reader's mind the image of a society up in shovels, bullwhips, cudgels, staves, and pikestaffs (but never arms—the rednecks and hayseeds mustn't be given bad ideas) against itself in scenes evoking Paris during the French Terror, but on a continental scale, from the White House to the California legislature in Sacramento. This, mind you, from people who accuse Donald Trump, the Republican Party, and conservatives generally of "dividing" and "polarizing" the country, and of encouraging a climate of "hate" and violence.

If the media, and the liberal institutions that support, abet, enable, and encourage them, are sincere in claiming that their aim is to "unify" the country by discouraging and prosecuting "hate" and "harmful" language, their fondness for colorful terms useful in enhancing stories about gang warfare in Chicago, Baltimore, and Long Island seem self-defeating at best.

Of course, they are not sincere about this. Their ambition is not for a unified United States but a country they have helped to sunder into two nations, for the purpose of destroying one of them. It is an ambition they are well on their way to achieving, even if it were well under way from the start.

5. Liberalism and America: Decline to Normal

The decline of once great powers, real and perceived, is a major theme of the early 21st century that is likely to become more pronounced as the century progresses and the balance of power, propelled by the shifting balance of energy and influence, shifts from West to East.

On the eve of the Second World War, the great Western powers were Great Britain, France, Germany, the Soviet Union, and the United States. Three quarters of a century later, the British are painfully aware of their diminished status in the world: the loss of empire, their vastly reduced army and almost nonexistent navy, their loss of political and economic influence on the Continent, and the weakening—accelerated by the Biden administration—of the Anglo-American alliance on which they relied for more than a century. The French (the French people) are dismayed by the loss of *gloire* and of empire, their subjugation by the European Union, the Americanization of classical French culture, mass immigration from the Third World, and the Islamization of France. The Russians, while pretending to accept Vladimir Putin's pretence of the resurrection of the Czarist empire, must be aware that their country in fact is headed for economic, cultural, and demographic disaster. The Germans, as everyone (including especially the Germans) expected they would, have regained in an astonishingly short time their pre-war status as the powerhouse of Europe, but they have yet to recover their moral and cultural self-confidence, though they are beginning to work on that, too. And in 2016 the United States experienced an election campaign that, despite the Republican candidate's emphasis on "Making America Great Again," focused on the need to shorten the country's global reach, to look out for herself as her first priority, and to reject what liberals here and abroad call her "international responsibilities."

The thing seems incredible, but to anyone—not just in the United States but everywhere in the world—who grew up in the 1950s and since, the fact of American global supremacy continues to be taken for granted almost as a fact of nature, like solar-centrism. The Cold War, it is true, has been viewed since the collapse of the Soviet Union as the last bipolar era in history, when two colossi managed the balance of international power between them. But while the USSR, post-war, was a military superpower capable of inspiring fear and awe internationally, the 20th century was indeed the American Century. Though tyrants, mature and budding, admired the Kremlin, their people did not, and no one aspired to the Soviet Way of Life. Rather all the world wished to be America, to paraphrase Locke, and America strove to be the world, realized in her own image. So superior did America—and Americans—appear that even those who resented and resisted her power acknowledged the superiority of the standard she represented, no matter whether they sought to attain it by different economic, political, and social means. Thus the American empire and imperial supremacy, to the astonishment of no one, became fixed in the world's eye as immutable, however unpleasant the prospect has seemed at times.

This was not the case with the modern empires that preceded it. The British Empire, which had reached its apogee by 1914, was the biggest thing of its kind the world had ever known: a vast arc of scarlet on the global map, arching north through Persia from its southwest anchor in South Africa to its southeastern one in the British East Indies. To build and support this arc, Britain willingly fought many wars on land and on the high seas, around the world and across four centuries. But Britain was never a Continental power in the sense that France, Spain, Portugal, Germany, and Austria were. For her, Continental allies and enemies were a means to securing and defending her non-European interests, in the Americas, in India, in Southeast Asia, and in Africa. As for her imperial rivals in Europe, the scope of their empires—even France's and Spain's—was narrower, in respect of the late colonial comers Germany and Italy especially. Even so British hegemony in 1914 fell far short of what the United States knew in 1945, to say nothing of what she has enjoyed since 1991. The collapse of the British Empire after 1945 was imaginable at the time to almost everyone but Winston Churchill. Today, though the decline of the American Empire over the past two decades is resisted by the popular imagination everywhere except in China, it is all too plausible to nervous imperialists with a stake in expanding it still further.

These include the politicians, the bureaucracy, the global capitalists, the military, and the international charitable enterprises—and they have reason to be nervous.

A present cause for alarm is Beijing's Asian Infrastructure Investment Bank and its enthusiastic acceptance by 57 founding members, including, to Washington's huge consternation, Britain, France, Germany, Australia, and Russia. The American enemies of the AIIB rightly see the project as a threat to the World Bank and the International Monetary Fund—both created at the Bretton Woods Conference in 1944, both based in Washington, D.C., and both traditionally headed by an American president—and thus to America's control of the global economy at a time when the future of the dollar as the world's dominant reserve currency is increasingly uncertain. In 1944, with the United States looming through the smoke of unfinished war as the coming world power, effectively giving Washington control of the global peacetime economy was sensible enough. Seventy-one years later it makes a great deal less sense, if indeed any sense at all, but liberal international politics resembles domestic liberal politics in a fundamental way.

Just as liberal government understands liberal institutions as established in perpetuity and beyond any chance of repeal, so it imagines the international status quo it has achieved as unchallengeable and immutable—*in seculae seculorum*—even while it hectors the governed to accept the fact that life itself is mutable and to "embrace change." Liberal government readily understands the proposition that a private citizen may possess too much money, power, and influence. It cannot fathom how government, supposing it to be at least ostensibly democratic, could have enough of all three. For government it is entirely natural, as well as eminently desirable, that the fortunes of individuals and families should fluctuate dramatically, Fate being the great equalizer across the decades, with a helping hand from the Internal Revenue Service. People must go down as well as up. Liberal nations and governments, on the other hand, must only go up and up and up, no matter whether their power and wealth are fairly shared by the people for whose benefit they supposedly exist, or not. For an American of the elite sort, America's right to preeminence in the world is ordained by the universe, the secular equivalent of the Divine Right of Kings. He has spent his entire life in that universe, and he cannot imagine life in any other. His personal failure to go on rising would signal national decline and fall. In fact, every serious student of history understands that America's status—political, military, and economic—in the world since 1945 is an historical anomaly, unnatural, unsustainable, and undesirable for everyone, and that the result of Washington's insistence on increasing it further is more likely Armageddon than the world transcendence Washington so confidently expects.

Great Britain destroyed her empire, and came close to destroying herself, in her obsession—raised by Churchill to a species of madness—with holding onto India, for whose sake she sacrificed a rational and responsible foreign policy and finally a sustainable economic policy as well. Franklin Roosevelt recognized this folly, and worked to take advantage of it. Without exception, his successors in the White House from 1945 to 2017 pursued variant forms of his strategy to convert British imperial power to American hegemony, while trying to avoid the fatal risks and responsibilities of a formal and direct empire. But responsibilities and burdens too are inevitably involved in indirect imperial power; and with them the unfathomable complexities, implacable contradictions, and sheer impossibilities. In Britain's ascendancy, Edmund Burke recognized some of them and urged his country to realize her limitations and to act realistically, in India and—especially—North America. Parliament, Burke insisted, could not bring the thirteen colonies to heel, regulate their economies, and take a profit from them, and it shouldn't try. Instead, it should recognize the facts for what they were and back away graciously, hoping to retain the colonists' good will and respect and engage in lucrative trade with them in future. But Parliament, save only for Burke's Rockingham faction, would have none of it, and the consequences were what Burke had predicted they would be. More importantly still, he perceived a connection between corruption in India and hubris in North America and political corruption and unconstitutional government at home, the land of Magna Carta and the Mother of Parliaments, as King George III and his shadow cabinet encroached on the rights of Parliament, and provoked the popular reaction Burke foresaw and feared would lead to political confusion and anarchy. (Owing partly to the Continental Army's victory over the British forces and the subsequent example of revolution, anarchy, and tyranny in France, this did not happen.)

American supremacy in 1945 was not, contrary to Marxist historians, won by an evil alliance of capitalists, militarists, and imperialists. Neither was it bad thing but a good one, for the world if not for the United States in the long run. In that year, and for a decade and a half afterward, American power and influence were actually providential, though the French refused to see the situation that way and the British resented it, while taking what advantage from it they could. From 1945 until about 1960, American hegemony was a healthy phenomenon because it was a natural one. President Eisenhower knew this. He also sensed that hegemony was approaching its natural and proper limits, as his warning against the "military-industrial complex" suggested. Even as he spoke, the presidential campaign of 1960, conducted mainly on the issues of the missile gap, the arms race, falling dominos, and "losing" countries to the enemy, suggested the unwillingness of the American political and managerial classes to countenance a return to a more natural distribution of international power and influence, in what was then called the Free World especially. It was at the tail end of Eisenhower's second administration that Washington began to locate Vietnam in its sights. During the Kennedy Administration it learned to keep them fixed there, and Johnson's White House pulled the trigger. The escalation of the Vietnam War marks the point at which American hegemony succumbed to American hubris—hegemony unsupported by power, logic, or common sense—while America's eventual withdrawal from the country represented the tactical retreat of the hegemonists that failed to conceal the underlying resentful grudge. Never mind the cliché that the United States had "learned a lesson." Washington had learned nothing, merely backed off from its aggressive global ambitions to bide its time, restore its treasury and its credibility, and wait to fight another day.

That day came in December, 1991, with the dissolution of the Soviet Union. Since then the U.S. has ceaselessly committed herself to a series of hot wars (all of them undeclared and all of them failures) fought to impose "democracy" on unwilling countries around the world, to an international propaganda campaign quieter, though perhaps even more intensive, than that waged by Radio Free America and other federal agencies during the Cold War, and to a shameless ideological assault on Russia meant to humiliate and bully that country into transforming herself in the image of the American liberal regime. Washington has further arranged that military and political intervention have been accompanied by commercial self-interpolation and exploitation—that American trade should follow U.S. forces and American "nation builders," social workers, and lawyers for an army of liberal NGOs—and that multi-national "free trade agreements" should be more or less mandated by American politicians to bundle all their efforts together into a giant fasces in the name of the "indispensable," the "exceptional," nation. America in the 21st century recalls Chesterton's rebuke of the Duke of Devonshire, in his day the richest man in England. The Duke with his vast holdings, Chesterton said, was like a man whose wealth allows him to maintain a household of fifty thousand wives, 49,999 of whom would otherwise belong to as many other men—an arrangement as unnatural as it is morally wrong. The decline of the United States from the status of sole superpower and indispensable nation, Lord of the World, is as natural and desirable as was her temporary preeminence following the Second World War.

This return to balance promises as much for America—meaning Americans themselves—as it does for the rest of the world. The hegemon by Acton's definition is corrupt, and republican government and corruption do not comport well. The more power our "leaders" exert over the world, the more power they claim over us, and the more high-handedly and carelessly they wield it. The more incompetently, too. American government in the 21st century finds almost everything she sets her hand to finally beyond her powers of accomplishment, while wreaking massive damage in the process: the inevitable result of trying to play God. Stalin corrected an emissary of Hitler's after he remarked that people don't know when to stop. "I do," Stalin told him. He didn't really; but we shall learn, in time, whether Donald Trump and his successors in the White House are as wise as Stalin thought he was.

The sun never set on the British Empire, the nanny never sleeps in what remains of Franklin Roosevelt's. Suns, however, do die, nanny's charges grow up eventually, and the old girl herself is relieved of her responsibilities and dismissed from service. Which is how life goes, and how it should go.

6. Unhappy Liberalism

Mass shootings, whose only conceivable motive seems to be the perpetrator's compulsion to make his satanic and nihilistic hatred of other people and of existence itself a compelling item in the international news, have become almost monthly occurrences in the United States, though they are rare in more mentally and emotionally healthy societies. Other Western countries, cultural cousins to the United States, face social challenges of their own, while sharing many of the pathologies that are presently consuming America. Nevertheless school killings, like mass slaughter of any kind, are not among them—murderous rampages by Third World immigrants and terrorists excepted. The reasons for the discrepancy are not immediately obvious, but a broad explanation may be that the U.S. is ground-zero for the explosion of post-modernity. Atrocities such as those in Parkland and Las Vegas, like the Columbine massacre of two decades ago, are not features of happy societies. They indicate that the United States is not only the wealthiest and most comfortable society in the world, but the unhappiest one as well. How can this be?

All people in every time and of every culture have wished to be happy. The urge to happiness is humanity's fundamental instinct after the urge to self-survival and self-reproduction, itself a type of happiness however spasmodic. But only Americans have lived for a quarter of a millennium under a guarantee of "the pursuit of happiness," a phrase invented by the most ideological president of the U.S., after Barack Obama, that can easily, and fatally, be misunderstood as a guarantee of happiness. In a recent book about the friendship between John Adams and Thomas Jefferson, the historian Gordon Wood observes that in Adams' mind the founding of the American Republic was an exercise in creating a new government, while for Jefferson it was the founding of a new age for mankind. This sort of millennial thinking, whether conscious or not among Americans of that period, and their happy awareness of their innumerable natural resources and of the vast spaces of a seemingly unlimited continent stretching westward beyond the Appalachians and the Alleghenies to another great ocean whose existence seemed almost a matter of faith, were a large component of the famous American spirit of indomitable optimism in a free and prosperous future, more abundant than any country had previously enjoyed and endowed with a degree of political and individual freedom unprecedented in history. Any approximation of this spirit was unknown in Europe before the French Revolution—the same old Europe that American democrats scorned and despised for its supposed tyranny, and for a deep strain (or stain, as Americans saw it) of pessimism drawn from millennia of experience and from a religion that promised Christians trial and suffering in this world, and happiness only in the next. Americans, as much as Europeans, were raised on books of prayer and devotion which taught that the easiest way to find happiness is to forget that any such thing exists, while the most difficult means to attain it is to seek it directly.

But in America, following the Wesleyan revival, the Protestant churches, liberalizing their doctrine as they accommodated themselves to the new democratic and positivistic society, began to lose sight of this lesson during the course of the 19th century. Today Christianity is far weaker in Western Europe than it is in America, where the Christian presence, though shallow, is nevertheless wide. This should give Americans an edge on happiness over the Europeans, but plainly it doesn't. Europeans in the past two centuries have grown increasingly materialistic and selfish (as the novels of Dickens and Balzac, for instance, demonstrate), but "happiness" for them has always been an abstract quality and therefore far less a goal than the political and social "equality" their political philosophers and other writers have offered them, while neglecting to mention "happiness" or its pursuit altogether. (There is no such thing as the "European Dream"—or the British, or the French, or the Italian, or the Spanish, or the German— of an ever-better future, the firm expectation of an ever-improved standard of living and contentment.)

Europe and America both are decadent societies, but they are decadent in their own ways. European decadence is the decadence of a civilization dying by degrees by its own hand, a suicide acting in slow motion that knows nevertheless how to die gracefully and even elegantly, surrounded by the glories, beauties, and appurtenances of the past, the old civilization it created over thousands of years. American decadence is an act of cultural violence, the sudden brutal replacement of a wan version of the European civilization, which America had neither the genius nor the time required to match, with an arrogant post-modern anti-civilization that is technologically progressive but socially and culturally regressive to the point of barbarism. The new liberal anti-civilization values (after the technological accomplishments that made it possible) happiness gained through absolute freedom of the self and the exaltation of the individual and his "rights," his opportunities for "self-realization," his ability to be whatever he wishes to be at any given moment, his freedom from social and governmental restraint, from the constraints of biological identity, of the supposedly unenlightened past, and—above all—of religion and the God he once accepted as being infinitely his superior and his Master. The post-modern American's obsession with securing absolute happiness corresponds with his equally obsessive concern with ceaseless "progress," making him vulnerable to promises by demagogic politicians of "hope" and of the "change" he imagines will reward "hope." The question of why the citizens of the wealthiest and "freest" country in the world should be so impatient with the comfortable present, so impatient for "change" (whose nature everyone is careful not to specify), and therefore in need of "hope" is a question no one ever thinks to raise.

It is a significant question nonetheless, the answer to which is post-modern liberalism's ideological commitment to a society totally mobilized to achieve its goal of transcendental perfection on earth. The same ambition was rampant in America around the middle of the 19th century, though in less bizarre and more rationalized forms in the early 20th. It has returned with a vengeance since the 1980s with a program that is at once exaggeratedly rationalistic and hopelessly fantastical. Liberalism, which has controlled America's principal institutions and American culture for the past century, never ceases dwelling on the unfairness, the inequality, and the incompleteness of American society past and present, and on how much "work" remains to be done to realize the glorious nation heralded by the Declaration of Independence. It is the self-serving argument of people who are working to transform the nation according to their vision for it and hand it over to the Democratic Party, the NGOs, the universities, and the other established liberal institutions. Nevertheless it is repeated so ceaselessly, ubiquitously, and shrilly that it has impressed itself on the minds of everyone exposed to it—including conservatives and other anti-liberals who have not been able to resist being unconsciously influenced by its siren song.

In the beginning, Americans pursued happiness through the political efforts of free men—working through representative government, the laws of free speech, and "democratic" institutions—acting freely. This was in the Constitutional and early Republican periods. Next they tried chasing happiness down in material ways: exploiting their natural resources, ensuring economic freedoms at home, and adopting protectionist policies abroad. During the second half of the 19th century they looked for happiness in "a more perfect union" by conquering and outlawing disunion, and in industrial development and empire. In the new century their way, their truth, and their life was a refurbished democratic system, which politicians insisted could be secured and guaranteed only by making the world safe for democracy. Following the Great War they tried unrestrained capitalism, the mixed economy of the New Deal, the defeat of "international communism," and finally global hegemony. So far, Americans had pursued happiness by hard application to material and human reality and its laws, while priding themselves on their realism, their common sense, their hard-headedness, their practicality, even their materialistic philosophy which they managed to reconcile to their satisfaction with their progressively attenuated, abstracted, and symbolic understanding of Christianity.

But then came the 1960s and a third American revolution, a revolution that was not narrowly political but fundamentally conceptual—a revolution that aimed to transform society, its moral, intellectual, and metaphysical bases, as steps in the "long march through the institutions" on the way to the political revolution that would inevitably follow. This new revolution—the work of the New Left proximately inspired by the immigrant Frankfurt School that stood behind it, though had it roots in American millennialism at least as early as the 18th century—coincided with an otherwise unconnected revolution: the digital revolution. With these the pursuit of happiness, which up until now had meant dominating and exploiting the material world, turned—like Dr. Johnson's seeker who, unable to draw truth from the cow, went to milk the bull—to the pursuit of unreality, and eventually to "virtual reality."

The revolt against the real—including natural law, human nature, the laws that govern human societies, the fact of there being two discrete sexes and the essential physical, mental, and emotional differences between man and woman, the historical truth of divine revelation, and so forth—inevitably brought immense social and moral confusion, in sexual and social relations especially. And the nearly simultaneous arrival of computers, the digital revolution, and virtual reality encouraged the abnegation of the real in every aspect and the collective escape into fantasy. The two combined made possible and allowed for biological and genetic engineering, "designer" babies, transsexual surgery that only the other day permitted transgendered "women" to lactate when presented with a biological woman's baby, and similar medical "advances," while creating the expectable metaphysical *angst* and moral confusion whose social effects include loneliness, uncertainty, fear, an absence of human grounding, and the spread of "lives of quiet desperation" from the artistic and intellectual classes to the masses, for which the evidence is apparent everywhere: mass murder, drug addiction, and the digital addiction that is producing mental, emotional, and physical pathologies among self-isolated young people especially, a considerable percentage of whom tell researchers that they have no close friends. (Astonishingly, people in the teens are giving up automobiles for the computer.) Last winter, Great Britain appointed a Minister for Loneliness to address the latter problem, one by no means confined to the young.

Post-modern liberal society's remedies for these evils are therapy: social and political therapy, "meaningful" political activism, social inclusiveness, more multiculturalism, more "caring," the further replacement of Christian morality by "ethics," and the expenditure of more public monies, psychotherapy, and "meds" to counter post-modern forms of addiction and the damaging effects of other "meds." All of them are wildly insufficient to treat the underlying problems, something that should be obvious to everyone and isn't. But liberalism has no other tricks in its medical bag.

Immediately after the latest shooting, liberals reflexively demand "gun control" and conservatives (just as reflexively) retort that "guns are not the problem." In fact there is no problem, and therefore no solution, available in the context of the social and mental world advanced liberalism has made. American society will either collapse in violence and chaos in the next couple of decades (perhaps much sooner), or it will heal itself by the rediscovery of sane thinking and a return to sane ways of life based on them, a process that is necessarily a gradual and prolonged one.

No Christian will ever be able to "prove" to the satisfaction of a follower of any other religion, of an agnostic, or of an atheist that Christianity is the "one true" religion, but it is relatively easy for him to show by resort to history that Christian societies have, on balance, been the most humane and civilized ones, while allowing that many societies ruled by false Christians have been despotic or simply brutal arrangements. American society in the 21st century is neither despotic (not yet, anyway) nor brutal, despite the murderous horror of abortion. It is, however, a profoundly neurotic society, deeply scored, crippled, and deformed by personal and collective neuroses whose origins one may easily trace. Chesterton, who once referred to what he called "the huge and healthy sadness" of the classical pagan world, glimpsed something of a future one in the rise of Nazism, which appalled and seems even to have terrified him though he died in 1936. What he foresaw was the huge unhealthy post-modern spirit that suffers from a desperation that is far deeper and more painful than sadness, even than death, and infinitely more demoralizing than both of them.

This unhappy desperation is liberalism's gift to humanity, the poisoned fruit that is slowly killing the giver along with the recipients.

7. Post-modern Liberalism: Politics Suspended

"Democracy Dies in Darkness" is the motto of the *Washington Post.* The editors of the *Post* belong to the honorable group of which Norman Podhoretz, the author and magazine editor, once confessed himself a member: Idolaters of Democracy. They also idolize big government, that implacable enemy of democracy, or so democrats believed before the 1930s. No doubt the editors could demonstrate to their own satisfaction and that of their readers how the two things are really compatible. They would have a harder job explaining why democratic government is imperiled by the lack of the "transparency" liberals demand in every part of its machinery and every nook and cranny of its being. To conservatives, always skeptical of governments of scale, more and evermore transparency should be good news, while for perspicacious liberals it should seem a danger. Yet for conservatives, who fear anarchy as much as tyranny, the possible paralysis of government functions should be a matter for concern.

"Nolite Confidere in Principibus"—"Do Not Put Your Trust in Princes"—is a guiding principle for people who believe that social and cultural problems do not have political solutions. Nevertheless, politics can cause social and cultural problems, exaggerate them, and hinder and prevent the development of solutions for these problems. Further, a dysfunctional political system is itself a social problem whose roots are frequently cultural and social. Yes, one ought not to trust in princes, but one can and should and must use them, curb them, and, occasionally, dethrone them. That kind of action necessarily entails imagining and implementing political means, and embracing political activity. The need for counter-political activity ("reactionary" politics, as liberals understand it when liberal institutions are dominant in society) implies a previous defeat for the traditional cultures conservatives defend, just as a hyper-politicized world represents a triumph for modern post-liberal culture.

Since the French Revolution, the left has been winning its war of 233 years against the right by elevating politics as the principal activity of modern Western societies, ahead even of commerce and professional sports, through the politicization of all human relationships, and of society itself. (The paradoxical truth that when everything is political, nothing is, is a pyrrhic one, either small comfort to anti-liberals or else irrelevant.) This politicization of society clearly demands a political strategy to reverse it: another paradox or contradiction and an equally unfortunate one, the vast majority of people being temperamentally unsuited to politicized existence as the history of societies ruled by ideological tyrannies shows. Advanced liberalism, which is wholly incompatible with the fixed human nature it denies, confronts mounting resistance in the 21st century by roughly fifty percent of the Western populations subject to the liberal regime. Under liberalism's sway cultural resistance is deliberately discouraged or simply outlawed by liberal governments, so the Resistance is inevitably a political movement. Government of the right kind, the proper size, and the appropriate limits is as necessary to the reestablishment and management of traditional societies as government of the wrong sort is to the continuation of liberal democracy. The idea that government is a necessary human institution is a truism, but one that bears repetition in the context of the claims of some contemporary conservatives that cultural renewal can be accomplished only at the local level and by traditional, nonpolitical institutions such the town councils, the churches, and the family, without reform of national politics and the federal government and perhaps without giving them much consideration.

No one disputes the fact that an open society and public government both—government proceeding substantially under the public gaze and in response to the will of the voting citizenry—are equally necessary to democracy; indeed, they *are* democracy. But government conducted openly in its broader operations is not the same thing as government conducted in the omnipresent glare of publicity and the media's piercing LED torch lights that penetrate everywhere by means of digital technology and whose discoveries are instantly disseminated far and wide and discussed and debated by journalists and other people in the hyperpartisan and hyper-emotional political atmosphere for which the extreme ideological divides in Western countries, the United States especially, are only partly responsible; the rest of it is attributable to endless reports of political and administrative minutia that partisans hope will ruin the electoral prospects of the political opposition. Politicians of the right and left praise transparency and encourage more of it when it helps them and their side, or cause, and denounce it and demand that it be thickened in the name of national security or whatnot when it compromises themselves. (Gerard Baker of the *Wall Street Journal* has noted that attacks from the left on what liberals call "disinformation" actually amount to attempts at suppressing one point of view.) But democracy is endangered as much by the light that blinds as it is by impenetrable darkness. And the first of these things is a greater threat to democracy in the digitalized 21st century than is the second.

As Macbeth murdered sleep, and the French Jacobins murdered politics in their day, the digital revolution has murdered public peace, public security, and—most of all perhaps—public certainty about anything at all. While the *Washington Post* frets about the onset of a new Dark Age bereft of democracy, the *New York Times* still prides itself after a century and a half on reporting "All the News That's Fit to Print." But today readers, even of the once-august *Times*, cannot be sure what is fit for print and what isn't, and one suspects that the paper's reporters aren't really sure either. Some item or another is excitedly reported and produces a brief and transient flurry of national attention before it is superseded and eclipsed in the public mind by another, very likely contradictory, something, or somethings. Transparency (or what gets passed off as the result of transparency) and the media glare endanger democratic society almost as much as they do democratic government. Popular "knowing" too much about too many things is far more subversive of democracy than knowing too little; the evil combination of transparency and digitalized communication is destroying the public understanding of what is going on in the public realm as surely as it is destroying the public peace.

The historian John Lukacs explained how what used to be called "public opinion" (the considered opinion of the educated elite) has disappeared almost entirely and been replaced by "public sentiment" (the unconsidered, unstable, ever mutable, and highly excitable feeling of the general public). Transparency is the creature of digital distraction and self-immersion in trivia shared by its dispensers as well as its consumers, whether public figures "in the know" or private individuals who never shook their congressman's hand. Democracy is—or is said to be, or supposed to be—government for, by, and of the people, but a people obsessed by fluff and their own emotional responses to negligible and false bits of "information," dishonestly as well as mistakenly disseminated (but who can tell the difference?), cannot be expected to participate responsibly or intelligently in the business of self-government.

Limitless "transparency," like limitless popular involvement, in government is a functional impossibility, as antidemocratic political theorists and philosophers and practicing politicians, to say nothing of professional diplomats, have recognized for millennia. An ideal whose realization is promised by a new generation of democratic office holders and public servants, transparency (reinforced as a virtue by the threat of ever more intrusive technology) has the dangerous effect of making citizens progressively distrustful of their elected and appointed public men and women in so far as they suspect they might not be keeping them informed of everything they have been taught to believe they have the right to be told about the workings of government and the public service, and thus increasingly frustrated, resentful, and unhappy with what they can manage to learn of public life. On the other side, transparency has encouraged honest politicians who fear they cannot effectively perform their legitimate duties in the harsh light of omnipresent scrutiny to become increasingly devious—or simply dishonest, or more dishonest—at work; behavior which, when finally disclosed, undermines further popular confidence in politicians, civil servants, and democratic politics and institutions themselves.

Underlying it all—extreme partisanship, scientific technique, and instant mass communication through personal devices as well as the mass media, their 24-hour news cycle and their insatiable hunger for hot stories and dramatic revelations, most of them ultimately trivial but always damaging to someone—lie the existential discontent and suspicion liberalism has instilled in the American and other Western publics with regard to their governments, their societies, and their condition in life. Westerners have learned to view contentment either as culpably reactionary or simply the lazy disposition of chumps who are willing to pretend they are not being had by "the system" while knowing that they really are. Liberal society is the first in history to mobilize itself on behalf of an agenda for solving "problems" instead of patiently coping with the conditions with which all human societies have always had to contend or adapt themselves to. Liberals understand society as a project to be realized at some infinitely receding point in the future, not the natural result of historical growth which they have neither the patience to understand nor the wisdom to respect. It is entirely to liberals' advantage to advance their program by encouraging people to form desires that cannot possibly be realized in this world (and in some cases shouldn't be in the next) and ask government to fulfill them directly, or face the consequences at the polls—or in the streets, a pre-technological mode of protest that has become wildly popular since Donald Trump was elected president in 2016. The mass march too has to do with transparency but transparency in reverse, the thing observed passing from the ruled toward the rulers rather than in the opposite direction. Even here, transparency avails government and society little, as the spectacle of a couple of million raucous and sloppy fat women enhancing the obscene spectacle of their outward physical persons with the scandal of their dress—pink pussy hats and vagina front-pieces—communicates precisely nothing beyond the fact that two million raucous and sloppy fat women, etc., etc. are unhappy with the way the world is, with the regard it has for them, and probably also with themselves. If that is transparency, so is a distortive mirror at a carnival reflecting loads of bussed-in freaks enjoying an outing from their institution.

What the *Post* calls "democracy" dies under many conditions. One of these is the condition of ignorance concerning what democracy is, and what it isn't.

Pierre Manent, in an essay "The Tragedy of the Republic" (*First Things*, May 2017), reminds us that the republican government in its true form is not, as moderns like to think, democratic but rather aristocratic. (Montesquieu described 17th and 18th century England as "a republic disguised under the form of monarchy.") Manent views the republic as "the regime that allows and encourages the most action." Following the line of argument he developed in a book of a few years ago, *Democracy Without Nations,* he asserts that, "Today we expect from a republic the opposite of a republic. We demand from it the least possible action, or what we call 'freedom.' For us, freedom is a world without command or obedience. It is a world in which public action can neither begin nor commend anything." This is so because democrats demand that their representatives and governments act as totally disinterested agents in their work of governance. No one who "serves" should take anything away from his service, they believe. But, Manent objects,

> Service to the republic cannot be disinterested, because it is paid for by what is most precious in the eyes of ambitious citizens, that is, the honors granted by the republic, which boil down to public esteem. It is not disinterestedness that we should be asking of those who govern us, but rather ambition. It has been too long since we had the rare benefit of being governed by truly ambitious statesmen. The conviction has taken hold that our regime would be more republican if it ignored political rule still more. Political leaders are to serve our interests rather than commend our collective actions. The reigning social philosophy postulates the power and self-sufficiency of a spontaneous social form that would bring together order and freedom without the mediation of political rule. This is to abandon society to its inertia, that is, its corruption.

And so:

> When one opens the polls to decide who will have the honor
> of not acting, rivalries can be lively and passions virulent, but
> the men and women who fear ruling all look alike. Paralysis
> and stasis are taking hold and sinking roots, with the fervent
> help of citizens who demand action—and protest at the first
> sign of it.

In Manent's insight we find at once the meaning of, and the explanation for, the passion of the democratic left for "transparency" in government, an obsession compounded of the popular jealousy and resentment of people in high places who stand to take something from their service while finding personal enjoyment and fulfillment in the exercise of the powers legally and constitutionally granted to them by the electorate. And when the people elected to "power" are as violently disliked by the political opposition as they are today, the jealousy and the resentment become literally uncontrollable. Trump, in the short run at least, stands to lose, not gain, financially from his four year term as the nation's Chief Executive, a fact that makes the Democratic representation of his connections and actions as a "conflict of interest" a hypocritical sideshow. Yet even in the absence of the former President's hostility toward Democratic "core values" and liberal "ideals," it is likely that whoever was elected to oppose Barack Obama would have been challenged (as Obama himself was, though mildly) by the organized ideological advocates of "transparency" which might be defined, to paraphrase Mencken, as the sick feeling that someone, somewhere in government is exercising public power to accomplish something necessary and important, and receiving his just reward for doing so.

8. Post-Liberal Politics

It is a healthy and encouraging sign when politicians don't know where they're going because they have no idea what's coming next, which pretty much describes the state of politics in the West today. Among the various political groupings, only liberals *really* know where they wish to go—

and that is simply where they've been going for the past few decades, charging ahead toward a world fully globalized through statism, open borders, neoliberal economics, identity politics, multiculturalism, secularism, science, and scientism: the politics of entropy. Their problem today is that they are no longer confident, and with good reason, of their ability to find sufficiently large constituencies to follow them in their flight into dystopia. Moreover they are being challenged from the further left by radicals—the "progressives"—who view them as the party of the post-modern establishment and for whom "liberal" is a slur word, while the so-called "populists," dreaded and despised by all true liberals, belong to the right *and* the left.

Conservatives, on the other hand, are not at all sure where they want to go, so long as it isn't toward liberalism. Their uncertainty ws reflected recently several years ago by reconsiderations in the philosophically opposed publications *Modern Age* and the *New York Times Magazine* of the nature and meaning of conservatism. This discussion is part of a debate in this country lasting a good three-quarters of a century and that has generally been long on academic theorizing and politicking, respectively, and short on conclusions that are clear-sighted, intellectually honest, and practical. (Frank Meyer's "fusionism," introduced in the 1950s by *National Review*, had been largely forgotten before *Modern Age* and Tevi Troy at the *Times* tried to resurrect it.) Chesterton said that the great distinction is not between liberal and conservative, but rather between wrong and right. This formula may seem to beg the question: By what standard is the "right" is to be judged? But it really doesn't. Indeed we all could have been spared the entire *liberal v. conservative* wrangle had conservatives conceded from the start the validity of the liberal charge against them: *viz.*, that they are, essentially, pre-modern people, meaning, pre-secularists, pre-capitalists, and pre-industrialists. This is not to say that conservatives since around the beginning of the 19th century have set their hand implacably against secularism, capitalism, and industrialism by refusing to recognize them, since to have done so would have changed them from conservatives into ideologues, their natural enemies. Yet conservatives should never forget where their social, intellectual, aesthetic, and moral homeland lies, and that is in the pre-modern era. (The vast majority of people we recognize as "liberals" and "conservatives" are really just plain liberals and conservative liberals.) Only once they have admitted the fact will they be in a position to discern and fix the difference between what they actually are and the circumstances history has decreed they must live and move in, and the materials with which they must work. This is why debates among conservatives about whether Donald Trump is, or is not, a conservative were simply a waste of everybody's time.

The liberals' problem is that they are really the sole ideological party remaining in the world today, while their enemies are almost entirely non-ideological; they are pragmatists. The 21st century is an anti-ideological century because it is an anti-intellectual century, despite (or because of) its being the first educational century, in which ideology is pretty well confined to the little worlds of academia, entertainment, and the media. The masses receive what they are encouraged to think of as "education," but which is really only "training" in a wide variety of trade, specialty, and technical schools. Accordingly, learned, philosophical, and even seriously thoughtful people are dismayingly rare. Liberals disdain "populists" for their academic ignorance and their lack of a social and political vision, partly because they are social and intellectual snobs, but also because the populists' want of an articulated political program makes it very difficult for liberal politicians to devise party agendas by which to appeal to, bamboozle, buy, and finally cheat them.

In America and Great Britain recently, voters have been breaking ranks all over the place, cross-voting, splitting their tickets, and abandoning party loyalties formed many generations ago and sustained up until now. In the wake of Theresa May's Folly in the summer of 2017, British journalists spoke of "consumerist" voting to gain one appealing item on the right, another desirable something on the left. And in France the same year the electorate (or the minority of it that voted in an election that saw the highest abstention rate since 1969) came together from every political direction to avoid any direction indicated by the leaders of the four long-established parties. Beyond that, in *La France* as in Britain and the U. S., voters seemed to want specific, practical, and tangible results while appearing oblivious, if not actually hostile, to theoretical considerations or any sort of political "philosophy." In fact their President of the past five years, Emmanuel Macron, has seemed uncertain whether he is a neoconservative, a neoliberal, or Napoleon Bonaparte reincarnated. That indeed is how people in the Western democracies have been trained to think, since that is how their "leaders" have imagined their states since the late 19th century: as elaborate political, bureaucratic, and corporate machines whose principal purpose is not governance in the traditional sense, but the steady production of goods and services for the benefit of the electorate and the creation of the sort of world liberal "leaders" wish to construct. Ultimately, their model for statesmanship is the international corporatist's model, the same model they accuse Donald Trump of looking up to.

"In the spirit of Jonathan Swift's 'Modest Proposal' there is a good deal to be said for nuclear war" is the first sentence of the first article in the Summer 2017 issue of the *Salisbury Review*. The last is "Anybody for *Enola Gay?*" The pair bracket a discussion by the editors of how the successes of applied science in recent centuries threaten to destroy the natural world and human civilization by human overpopulation, pollution, and other types of stress it brings to bear upon nature. This is true irrespective of the truth of the Church of Climatology's central teachings which, if there is any truth in them at all (as there surely is), do no more than provide a theoretical explanation for phenomena observed and reported for decades by ordinary people before "climate change" became a cultural cliché. The introduction of modern Western medicine to populations in the Third World increased those populations enormously. The population of Africa, for instance, is expected to double between now and 2050 on a continent whose climate is changing dramatically and for the worse, and whose inhabitants are conspicuously incapable of sustaining even pastoral economies, let alone constructing the political and social structures that make modern economies and societies possible. Modern technological advances, in social communications and transport especially, make primitive populations painfully aware of the contrasting reality of the prosperous Western countries and offer them relatively cheap and easy means to travel there. Population increase and the correspondent scarcity of resources in poor non-Western countries promote tribal and regional warfare. So do the social networks created by Western technology which, contrary to liberal fantasy, alienate cultures from one another to a far greater degree than they bring them together, thus creating rivals and enemies instead of friends. It is true that as poverty increases in some parts of the world, wealth also does—and with wealth, pollution. "As wealth increases," the *Review* notes, "so does industrial output, with its attendant miseries of mass consumerism, social breakdown, tourism, cars, aircraft, noise, roads, television, the mobile phone and Everests of rubbish. As wealth increases so their production and consumption will increase. What will the world look like when one in every four people of the seven billion now alive owns a car and has a bit of road to drive on?" Owing to all these factors—climatic, economic, political, and technological—more refugees, displaced persons, and migrants (and terrorists, under cover of their numbers) are on the move around the world than at any time in history, ensuring collisions of people and civilizations on an increasingly vast scale in future decades. The untitled leader is followed directly by *"Auf Wiedersehen, Deutschland"* whose author, Paul Weston, concludes that "Demographics are destiny and Germany's tragic destiny, if nothing is done to halt it, is inevitably Islamic." In other words: Germany is finished.

I do not believe the *Salisbury Review* exaggerates either the present or the probable future state of the world—the West and the rest. All of us are confronted by a world beset by so many confluent and immediate crises arising from the contradictions of modern civilization that political philosophy may have become simply irrelevant and politics reduced to a series of *ad hoc* and more or desperate grapplings with cascading events, as in wartime, that will continue for the indefinite future. The world appears to face, in addition to the terrorism with which we have all become too familiar, the arrival of a formless, shapeless, intermittent, and undeclared world war from which the belligerents retire occasionally and which they rejoin intermittently, as they feel the need to do. "We fight not against organized ideologies but against fundamental chaos," the historian Bradley J. Birzer wrote recently in *Modern Age*.

Confronted by this fact, the left is not going to surrender. It is not even going to change, unless compelled to do so. It will remain imperviously and irrationally ideological until it "runs out of road" and implodes. The alternative to leftism is probably not some form of rationalized self-conscious conservatism based upon "our philosophy" and "our principles," as these were smugly invoked by the Republican establishment before it was routed in the primaries and the general election of 2016.

Instead it will likely be the anti-liberalism, plain and simple, that raised Donald Trump to the presidency. That is what increasingly large numbers of Americans and Europeans seem to want: a non-theoretical, non-ideological form of politics that in the case of the United States may be out of patience even with constitutionalism, or at least the sort of constitutionalism that is based on the existing U. S. Constitution. If that should really be the case, then the country will become truly ungovernable and democratic government will be replaced by the authoritarian sort, something at least one of the Founding Fathers predicted would happen a century out from the Constitutional Convention of 1787.

The great question is what might follow should the political movement loosely called Trumpism "fail," whatever failure might mean. The answer is probably one of two things: the continuation of highly practical politics along somewhat altered lines or the replacement of pragmatism by a vaguely theological orientation, no matter how weakly and imperfectly it represented traditional Christianity, or "progressivism," the latest euphemism for "socialism." This latter trajectory is not unknown to history in times of previous crisis, spiritual confusion, uncertainty, and fear. In any event, liberalism is not going to collapse in the near future. It will be with us for some time yet, prolonging the domination of a political establishment that promotes an aggressively and scrupulously secular identity while having, as Chesterton said of America, the heart of a church. The maxim that it takes one to know one suggests that it takes one to beat one as well. In that case the Phoenix that is Christ, disguised by glorious avian plumage exceeding the serpent Quetzalcoatl's in its finery, might arise triumphant from the ashes, and sooner perhaps than we think.

Other Works by Chilton Williamson, Jr.

Nonfiction:
The Immigration Mystique: America's False Conscience
The Conservative Bookshelf
After Tocqueville: The Promise and Failure of Democracy

Narrative Nonfiction:
Saltbound: A Block Island Winter
Roughnecking It: Or, Life in the Overthrust
The Hundredth Meridian: Seasons and Travels in the New Old West

Fiction:
Desert Light
The Homestead
Jerusalem, Jerusalem!
Mexico Way
The Education of Héctor Villa
The Last Westerner (forthcoming)